THE KARNISCHER HÖHENWEG

About the Author

John Hayes is a retired management consultant with degrees from Liverpool University and University College London. Immediately after finishing work in 2011, he embarked on an epic 5000km trek across Europe, walking from Tarifa in Spain to Budapest. He first walked the Karnischer Höhenweg in 2012 as part of a hike along the Via Alpina, and was so impressed that he returned in 2015 and again in 2016.

John has written for numerous walking and trekking magazines. The Karnischer Höhenweg is his third guide for Cicerone.

Other Cicerone guides by the author
The GR1: Spain's Sendero Histórico
Trekking Munich to Venice

THE KARNISCHER HÖHENWEG

A 1–2 WEEK TREK ON THE CARNIC PEACE TRAIL: AUSTRIA AND ITALY

by John Hayes

JUNIPER HOUSE, MURLEY MOSS,
OXENHOLME ROAD, KENDAL, CUMBRIA LA9 7RL
www.cicerone.co.uk

© John Hayes 2018
First edition 2018
ISBN: 978 1 85284 942 9

Printed in Poland on behalf of Latitude Press Ltd
A catalogue record for this book is available from the British Library.

All colour photographs are by the author unless otherwise stated.
The World War I public-domain photographs are from the archives of the Österreichische Nationalbibliothek, made available through the Europeana Collections: www.europeana.eu/portal/en.

Route mapping by Lovell Johns www.lovelljohns.com
Contains OpenStreetMap.org data © OpenStreetMap contributors, CC-BY-SA. NASA relief data courtesy of ESRI

Updates to this guide

While every effort is made by our authors to ensure the accuracy of guidebooks as they go to print, changes can occur during the lifetime of an edition. Any updates that we know of for this guide will be on the Cicerone website (www.cicerone.co.uk/942/updates), so please check before planning your trip. We also advise that you check information about such things as transport, accommodation and shops locally. Even rights of way can be altered over time.

The route maps in this guide are derived from publicly available data, databases and crowd-sourced data. As such they have not been through the detailed checking procedures that would generally be applied to a published map from an official mapping agency, although naturally we have reviewed them closely in the light of local knowledge as part of the preparation of this guide.

We are always grateful for information about any discrepancies between a guidebook and the facts on the ground, sent by email to updates@cicerone.co.uk or by post to Cicerone, Juniper House, Murley Moss, Oxenholme Road, Kendal LA9 7RL.

Register your book: To sign up to receive free updates, special offers and GPX files where available, register your book at www.cicerone.co.uk.

Front cover: Descending from Pfannspitze towards Kleine and Große Kinigat on Stage 2

CONTENTS

Map key 7
Area map 9
Route overview map. 10–11
Route summary tables 12–13

INTRODUCTION 15
The Peace Trail 16
The route 17
World War I earthworks and remains 19
The landscape and views 21
Geology 22
Plants and wildlife 24
How hard is the walk? 25
Selecting an itinerary 26
Getting to and from the route 29
When to go 30
Accommodation and food 31
Budget 33
What to take. 34
Routefinding. 34
Safety and emergencies 36
Using this guide 36

THE ROUTE 39
Stage 1   Arnbach to Obstanserseehütte. 40
Stage 2   Obstanserseehütte to Porzehütte 55
Stage 3   Porzehütte to Hochweißsteinhaus 64
Stage 4   Austrian route: Hochweißsteinhaus to Gasthof Valentinalm. 75
Stage 4A   Italian route: Hochweißsteinhaus to Rifugio Marinelli 88
Stage 5   Austrian route: Gasthof Valentinalm to Zollnerseehütte 94
Stage 5A   Italian route: Rifugio Marinelli to Plöckenpass. 101
Stage 5B   Italian route: Plöckenpass to Casera Pramosio 106
Stage 5C   Italian route: Casera Pramosio to Zollnerseehütte 114
Stage 6   Zollnerseehütte to Nassfeld. 119
Stage 7   Nassfeld to Gasthaus Starhand 129
Stage 8   Gasthaus Starhand to Arnoldstein 139

Appendix A Route breakdown 146
Appendix B Accommodation 154
Appendix C Useful contacts 155

Mountain safety

Every mountain walk has its dangers, and those described in this guidebook are no exception. All who walk or climb in the mountains should recognise this and take responsibility for themselves and their companions along the way. The author and publisher have made every effort to ensure that the information contained in this guide was correct when it went to press, but, except for any liability that cannot be excluded by law, they cannot accept responsibility for any loss, injury or inconvenience sustained by any person using this book.

International Distress Signal *(emergency only)*
Six blasts on a whistle (and flashes with a torch after dark) spaced evenly for one minute, followed by a minute's pause. Repeat until an answer is received. The response is three signals per minute followed by a minute's pause.

Helicopter Rescue
The following signals are used to communicate with a helicopter:

Help needed:
raise both arms
above head to
form a 'Y'

Help not needed:
raise one arm
above head, extend
other arm downward

Emergency telephone numbers
The emergency telephone number for all Europe is 112.

Official national weather services
Austria – Zentralanstalt für Meteorologie und Geodgynamik www.zamg.at
Italy – Meteo Aeronautica www.meteoam.it

Note Mountain rescue can be very expensive – be adequately insured.

MAP KEY

Symbols used on route maps

~	route
---	alternative route
(S)	start point
(F)	finish point
(AS)	alternative start point
☁	glacier
◯	lake
	woodland
	village or town
	international border
▬━▬	station/railway
▲	peak
⬆ ⇧	manned/unmanned refuge
⇧	refreshments
■	building
✚	church or chapel
)(	pass or saddle
•	point of interest
───	cable car/ski lift
🚌	bus stop

Relief
in metres

- 5000 and above
- 4800–5000
- 4600–4800
- 4400–4600
- 4200–4400
- 4000–4200
- 3800–4000
- 3600–3800
- 3400–3600
- 3200–3400
- 3000–3200
- 2800–3000
- 2600–2800
- 2400–2600
- 2200–2400
- 2000–2200
- 1800–2000
- 1600–1800
- 1400–1600
- 1200–1400
- 1000–1200
- 800–1000
- 600–800
- 400–600
- 200–400
- 0–200

SCALE: 1:50,000

0 kilometres 0.5   1
0 miles   0.5

Contour lines are drawn at 25m intervals and highlighted at 100m intervals.

GPX files

GPX files for all routes can be downloaded free at www.cicerone.co.uk/942/GPX.

THE KARNISCHER HÖHENWEG

The World War I memorial on Freikofel summit dates from the 1920s (Stage 5B)

AREA MAP

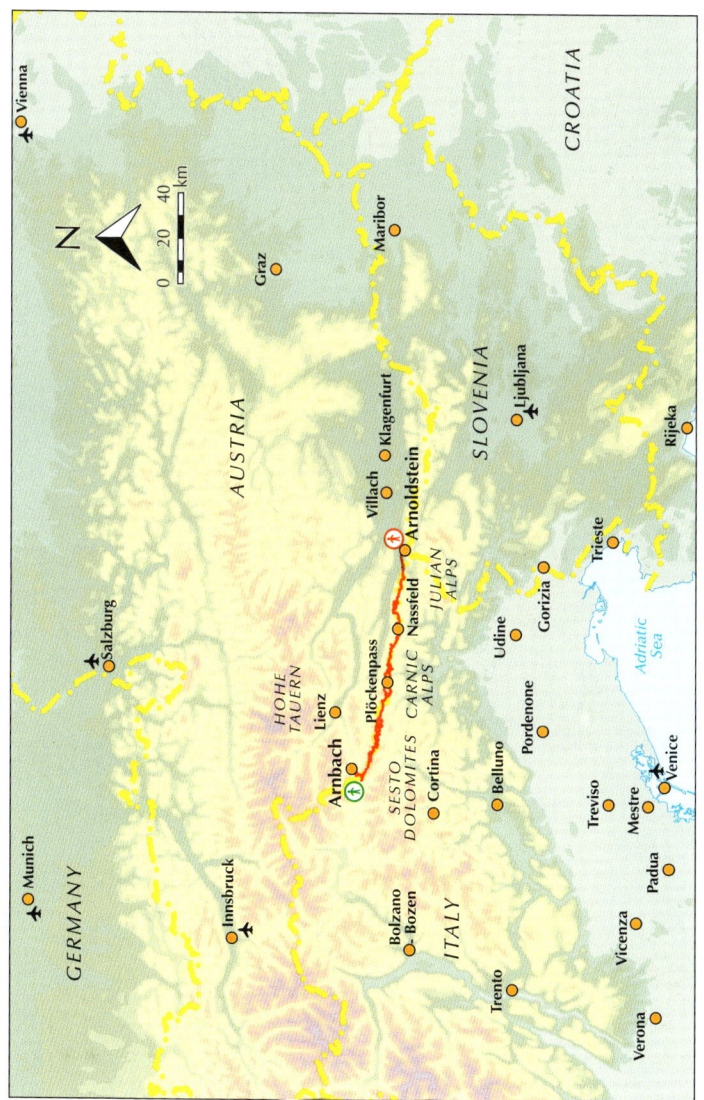

THE KARNISCHER HÖHENWEG

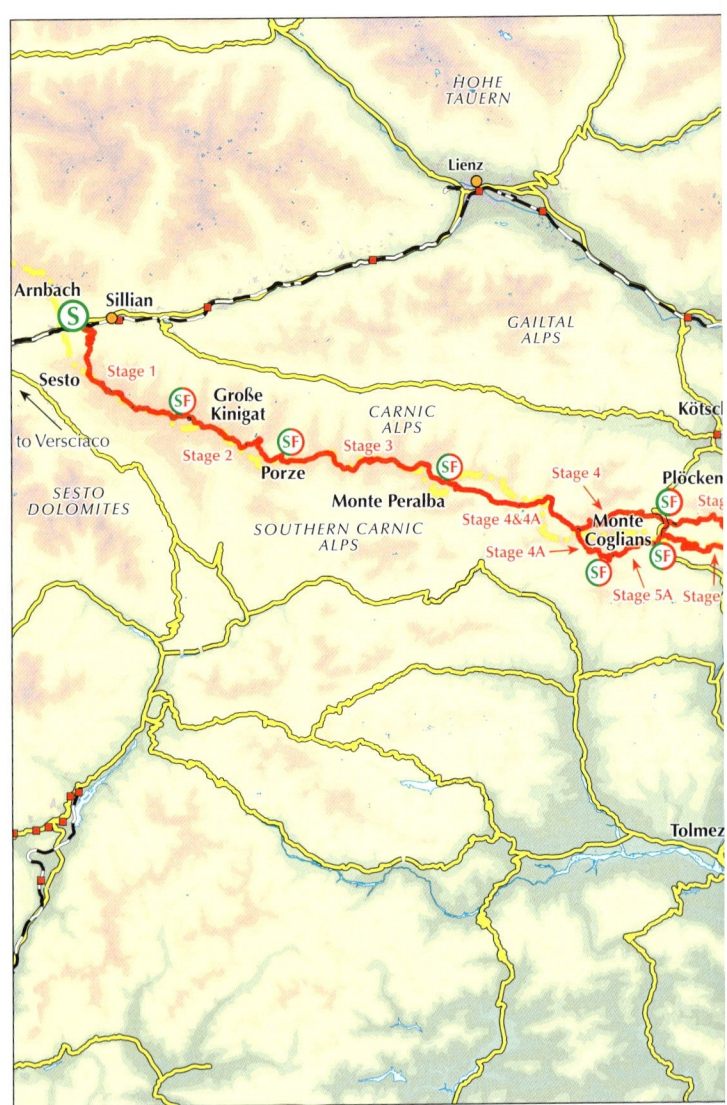

Overview map

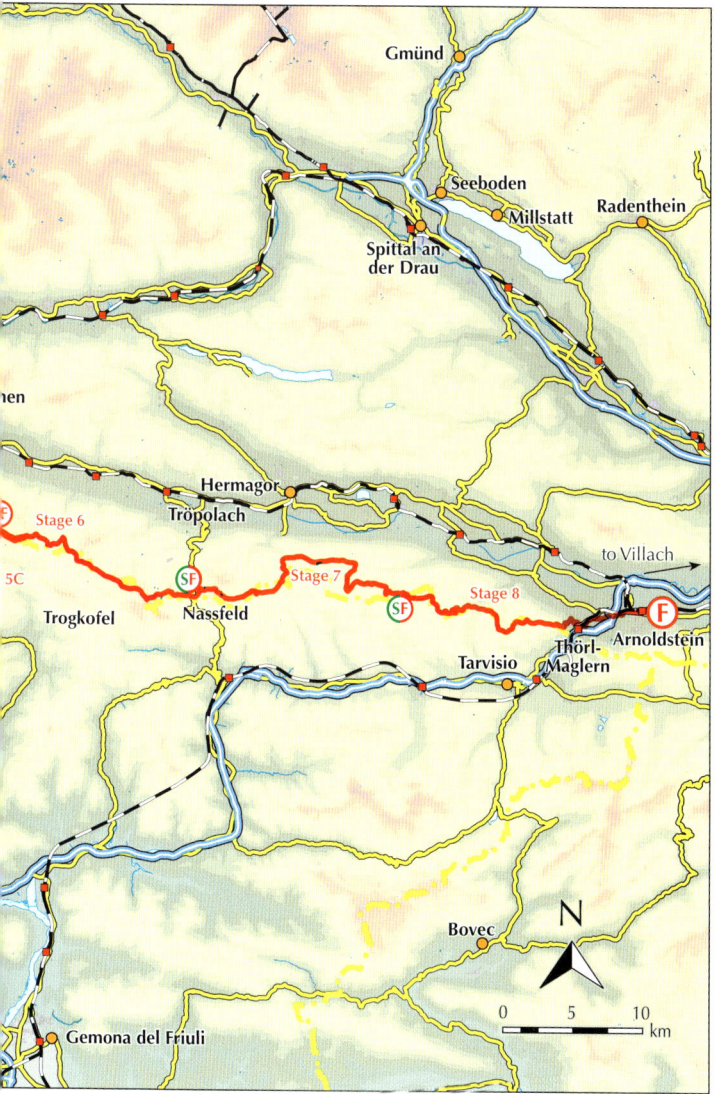

ROUTE SUMMARY TABLES

Austrian route – 8 days

Stage	Time	Distance (km)	Ascent/descent (m)	Notes	Page no
Stage 1: Arnbach to Obstanserseehütte	8hr 45min	18.3	1900/550	Consider taking ski lift	40
Stage 2: Obstanserseehütte to Porzehütte	6hr 30min	12.2	740/110		55
Stage 3: Porzehütte to Hochweißsteinhaus	8hr	17.8	1180/1240		64
Stage 4: Hochweißsteinhaus to Gasthof Valentinalm	9hr	23.2	1180/1820	Consider an extra day and stay at Wolayerseehütte	75
Stage 5: Gasthof Valentinalm to Zollnerseehütte	7hr 30min	19	1440/950		94
Stage 6: Zollnerseehütte to Alpenhof Plattner	8hr 20min	23.8	970/1080		119
Stage 7: Alpenhof Plattner to Gasthaus Starhand	8hr 20min	26.6	1100/1270	Consider an extra day and stay at Eggeralm	129
Stage 8: Gasthaus Starhand to Arnoldstein	8hr 30min	28	1100/1800		139
Total	**approx. 65hr**	**168.9**	**9610/8820**		

Other schedules are summarised in 'Selecting an itinerary' in the introduction to this guide.

ROUTE SUMMARY TABLES

Italian route – 10 days

Stage	Time	Distance (km)	Ascent/descent (m)	Notes	Page no
Stage 1: Arnbach to Obstanserseehütte	8hr 45min	18.3	1900/550	Consider taking ski lift	40
Stage 2: Obstanserseehütte to Porzehütte	6hr 30min	12.2	740/110		55
Stage 3: Porzehütte to Hochweißsteinhaus	8hr	17.8	1180/1240		64
Stage 4A: Hochweißsteinhaus to Rifugio Marinelli	8hr 50min	19.9	1360/1100	Consider an extra day and stay at Rifugio Lambertenghi	88
Stage 5A: Rifugio Marinelli to Plöckenpass	2hr 15min	6.3	100/760	Consider climbing either Monte Coglians or Cellon	101
Stage 5B: Plöckenpass to Casera Pramosio	7hr 15min	11.2	1300/1030		106
Stage 5C: Casera Pramosio to Zollnerseehütte	3hr	7	700/500	Consider climbing Hoher Trieb	114
Stage 6: Zollnerseehütte to Alpenhof Plattner	8hr 20min	23.8	970/1080		119
Stage 7: Alpenhof Plattner to Gasthaus Starhand	8hr 20min	26.6	1100/1270	Consider an extra day and stay at Eggeralm	129
Stage 8: Gasthaus Starhand to Arnoldstein	8hr 30min	28	1100/1800		139
Total	**approx. 70hr**	**171.1**	**10,450/9440**		

THE KARNISCHER HÖHENWEG

Looking along the ridge from Pfannspitze (Stage 2)

INTRODUCTION

Don't be surprised to hear the Peace Bell being rung as you climb Monte Coglians (Stage 4A or 5A)

The Karnischer Höhenweg is a 169km long-distance trek along the main ridge of the Carnic Alps, a mountain range straddling the border between Italy and Austria. It's a beautiful high alpine walk, mostly above the tree line, with amazing views of the Dolomites to the south and the Hohe Tauern to the north. Although not particularly famous, the Carnic Alps have a unique history and geography, and walking there is a special experience.

The Karnischer Höhenweg follows the World War I front line, and reminders of the conflict that defined both Italy and Austria are everywhere. Although the fighting took place 100 years ago, the front line – marked out by trenches, dugouts and barbed wire – is still a distinct feature.

Perhaps less obvious is that the Carnic Alps are also the location for another important dividing line, the Periadriatic geological seam, which runs parallel to the range in the valley immediately to its north. This division between the African and European tectonic plates, as Africa continues its drive northwards, is key to understanding the origins of the Alps.

These dividing lines turn what would otherwise be just another wonderful stretch of alpine walking

The Karnischer Höhenweg

into something really special. One minute you're walking through classic limestone scenery (technically the Carnic Alps are in the Southern Limestone Alps) and the next you're among ancient schist and granite, in scenery more commonly found in the central core of the Alps. One minute you're in Austria and the next you're in Italy, and despite open borders, the cultures, like the geology, are very different.

The special nature of the Carnic Alps makes them a honeypot for hikers, and five different long-distance walks traverse them. In addition to the Karnischer Höhenweg and the Italian version, the Traversata Carnica, they are traversed by: the E10, one of Europe's 12 long-distance hikes; the Via Alpina, the main red route on its way from Monaco to Trieste; and the 03, the Südalpenweg, one of Austria's 11 national trails.

THE PEACE TRAIL

The mountain fighting in World War I lasted for just two and a half years, from May 1915 to October 1917, but its impact, both culturally and physically, endures. The immediate post-war period saw ethnic cleansing, a hardening of the borders and, on the Italian side, a concerted process of 'Italianisation' – the imposition of the

Watch out for the memorial to the founder of the Peace Trail near the Hintersattel (Stage 2)

Italian language. The bitterness provoked by this process was deep and, some argue, still persists.

The Peace Trail and much of the early promotion of the Karnischer Höhenweg is down to the work of ex-army officer, alpinist and historian Walther Schaumann. The son of a soldier who had served in World War I, Walther believed that restoring wartime relics and making them accessible to visitors was an important act of reconciliation. He coined the term 'Peace Trail', which now applies to three routes: the first part of the Karnischer Höhenweg, established by the Dolomitenfreunde (Friends of the Dolomites) in Austria; the Itinerari di Pace sul Carso della Grande Guerra in Italy; and the Pot Miru (Walk of Peace) in Slovenia.

Walther Schaumann founded the Dolomitenfreunde in 1973 with the aim of supporting peace and international understanding through research and documentation of the former conflict areas. The main activity was turning 'war trails' – the routes formerly used to supply troops – into 'peace trails'. Each summer, volunteers from all over the world gather to carry out this work. The motto of the Dolomitenfreunde is 'Trails that used to separate the front lines nowadays connect us.' As well as creating some 300km of peace trails, the association has established outdoor museums at Plöckenpass and Monte Piana and an indoor museum at Kötschach-Mauthen.

THE ROUTE

The Karnischer Höhenweg follows the Carnic Alps and is traditionally walked from west to east, from Sillian through to Thörl-Maglern (although to find easy transport the guide recommends extending the walk a few kilometres to Arnoldstein). The mountain range is long and thin, and generally speaking both the route and the border between Austria and Italy follow the central ridge. The range is intersected by two significant passes, the Plöckenpass and the Nassfeldpass, both of which are important north–south transport links. Generally the route stays high, at between 2000 and 2500m. The first two-thirds are alpine in character, with spectacular walking, consistently above the tree line. The final third is more pastoral, with meadows, cows and trees.

The route can be completed in 8–10 days, although, given the amount there is see, most people will take longer. In particular, there are alternative routes around Monte Cogliáns, the highest mountain of the Carnic Alps. The original route (referred to in this book as the 'Austrian route') can be completed in 8 days; it stays to the north of Monte Cogliáns. The southern route (presented here as the 'Italian route') requires 10 days and is more challenging than the Austrian route.

See also 'Selecting an itinerary' below for two alternative options: an 8-day trek taking in the highlights of the Karnischer Höhenweg; and a more leisurely 12-day trek.

The Karnischer Höhenweg

WORLD WAR I EARTHWORKS AND REMAINS

In the Carnic Alps, the World War I front line coincides with today's border between Austria and Italy, and generally speaking the border follows the watershed. Where the ridges are long and sustained, the trench lines are easy to spot because they are almost invariably orientated to the south (the Austro-Hungarians established their defensive positions first). In the more mountainous parts of the route, the location of the front line is sometimes harder to identify, but all the mountaintops are fortified and here the remains are typically extensive.

The visible evidence of the war is everywhere. As well as trenches and protective earthworks, tunnels were hacked into the sides of mountains, sometimes extending from one side to the other. Command posts, cooking stations and latrines can be found, along with rotting floor and roofing materials. Coils of rusting barbed wire, still where they were positioned over a hundred years ago, are everywhere. Occasionally a brass button or a strip of shoe leather acts as a more intimate reminder, if needed, that men actually lived and fought on the mountaintops.

Moving a field gun at Filmoorhöhe (Stage 2); Observation post on Eisenreich (Stage 1); Trenches on Kleiner Pal (Stage 5B); Naval gun at Straniger Alm (Stage 6) (public-domain photographs taken from the archives of the Österreichische Nationalbibliothek)

Less immediately apparent than the remains on the front line are what's left of the transport infrastructure developed to supply it. At the beginning of the campaign, all the materials were carried up to the front line by pack ponies, dogs and men (often prisoners), so any zigzag trail working its way up the mountainside (sometimes all that's left is the outline on the hillside) is likely to have been constructed for this purpose. Some of the routes are particularly elaborate and involved significant works of construction and engineering. Later in the campaign, the infrastructure became more sophisticated, and the technological advances involved, including cable cars, were used after the war to develop the skiing industry.

The World War I Open-air Museum at Plöckenpass is particularly interesting. Here, the Dolomitenfreunde have restored an area that, because of the pass, was particularly heavily defended. Both the Austrian and Italian front lines, which here were only 30 metres apart, can be visited. It is not a museum in the conventional sense, there are no entry and exit points and the curation is minimal, but after days of walking through war remains it's easy for your imagination to fill in the gaps.

Where it can, the route follows the border and the front line. The bigger mountains, however, are typically circumvented either to the north or south. Nearly all these mountains can be easily climbed and the crowning fortifications visited.

THE KARNISCHER HÖHENWEG

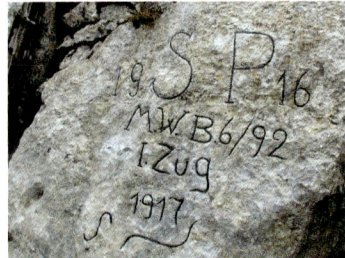

THE LANDSCAPE AND VIEWS

SUGGESTED READING

- *The White War: Life and Death on the Italian Front, 1915–1919* by Mark Thompson
- *The War that Ended Peace* by Margaret MacMillan

THE LANDSCAPE AND VIEWS

The Karnischer Höhenweg is a ridge walk and the views in all directions are often spectacular. It sits right in the middle of some huge mountain ranges. The views to the south, particularly at the beginning of the walk, are dominated by what is arguably the most beautiful part of the world's most beautiful mountain range, the Sesto Dolomites. To the north, the much smaller Lienz Dolomites (the western end of the Gailtal Alps) attempt to grab attention, only to be put firmly in their place by the more distant but much larger white-topped summits of the Hohe Tauern. Views of Austria's most important range, dominated by its highest mountains the Großglockner (3798m) and the Großvenediger (3764m), can be seen along the entire length of the Karnischer Höhenweg. To the south, views of the Sesto Dolomites are replaced by the South Carnic Alps, a complex range of limestone mountains dissected by deep valleys. The Julian Alps, Slovenia's most important mountain range, come into view from

Field kitchen on Kleiner Pal (Stage 5B); Insignia carved into rocks; All-too-real dugout on Große Kinigat (Stage 2)

the southern side of Monte Coglians on day 4 and, like a harbinger of the journey's end, dominate the second half of the Höhenweg.

The landscape changes as the Karnischer Höhenweg journeys from west to east. Until Nassfeld, it is alpine in character and features massive limestone peaks and long ridges of granite and gneiss. After Nassfeld, and dropping down a little, forests dominate and here the highlights are the little hamlets, occupied only in the summer, dedicated to the production of cheese.

The highest point on the route is Pfannspitze (2678m), a granite mountain climbed on the second day. There are, however, a series of optional climbs, some of which, if the weather is good, will be irresistible to those with time. These include some of the highest mountains of the Carnic Alps, the massive limestone lumps of Monte Coglians (2789m), Monte Peralba (2694m), Große Kinigat (2689m) and Trogkofel (2279m).

The limestone stretches of the Höhenweg are the most dramatic, characterised by towering cliffs, steep banks of tumbling scree, and dry valleys. Although less dramatic, the gneiss landscapes provide the best

The Karnischer Höhenweg

The silhouette of the Julian Alps from the unnamed pass near Ringmauer (Stage 6)

walking. Here, the ridges are more sustained, and the hillsides, particularly those facing south, are grassier.

GEOLOGY

Some argue that the Carnic Alps, from a geological perspective, are the world's most interesting mountain range. They are designated, along with the Gailtal Alps, as a UNESCO Global Geopark.

The geological boundary between the African and European tectonic plates, the Periadriatic seam, runs along the valley immediately to the north of the Carnic Alps. In a simple world, this would have provided the dividing line between mountains to its north, dominated by the granite and gneiss of the Hohe Tauern, and mountains to the south, the limestone of the Dolomites. However, although the Carnic Alps are on the southern side of the dividing line, they don't just consist of limestone but also include the granite and gneiss of the Hohe Tauern.

The area was covered twice by the sea for hundreds of millions of years. The first of these seas covered today's Carnic Alps in the Ordovician age, during which sediments were formed. Then 440 million years ago an 'event' triggered the first build-up of mountains in the area and an igneous plate was pushed over the sedimentary rocks. The remains of this plate can be seen in several places on the main Carnic Alps ridge.

GEOLOGY

Some 350–400 million years ago, and after erosion had removed most of the mountains, a second sea (the Thetis Sea) covered the area for some 200 million years. This enabled the formation of incredibly thick coral atolls, the remains of which are today's limestone mountains, including the Dolomites.

The final formation of the Alps began 200 million years ago, and here again the Carnic Alps are special. The mountains folded upwards and rolled northwards like waves breaking on a beach. (The geological term is 'nappe', from French *nappe*, a tablecloth, because of the way a tablecloth folds and crumples when it is pushed across a table.) With the waves breaking over the Periadriatic line, the layering of the rocks became more and more complicated. 'Suddenly' (in the geological timescale) old layers were sandwiched between younger ones, sometimes vertically, sometimes horizontally.

The Carnic Alps UNESCO Global Geopark is well resourced, with a visitor centre at Dellach and six geotrails – short walks featuring important geological features described with noticeboards. Four of these geotrails (Wolayersee, Plöckenpass, Zollnersee and Nassfeld) are close to the Karnischer Höhenweg. The Plöckenpass trail, near the World War I Open-air Museum, visits the Cellon avalanche gully, which features the world's longest *in situ* rock strata timeline.

Looking from the Luggauer Sattel to the intimidating cliffs of Torkarspitze (Stage 3)

PLANTS AND WILDLIFE

For most of its journey, the Karnischer Höhenweg stays high and travels through a landscape that for much of the year is covered in snow. Natural vegetation needs an ability to cope with low temperatures and make the best of a short growing season.

The edelweiss (symbol of both the German and Austrian Alpine Clubs), with its creamy felt-like petals in a star formation, may be the most famous flower, but it is only one of over 1500 species that can survive such alpine conditions. Easier to spot than edelweiss are blue trumpet gentians or harebells. Perhaps a little gaudy and much larger is the orange lily. You may also see, growing heroically on inhospitable limestone scree, the golden yellow Rhaetian poppy, the larger flowered ox-eye, or the globeflower. Common in damp valleys, and familiar to English walkers from the Pennines, are the tufty flowers of cotton grass. Attractive even to those with the most casual interest in flowers are orchids, the most spectacular of which is probably the lady's slipper orchid with its maroon and yellow petals. Also featured are the alpenrose, of which there are at least two common varieties: the red-flowered auburn alpenrose, and the hairy alpenrose, which has pinker flowers. The mauve-flowered Wulfenia, a member of the plantain family, is unique to the Nassfeld area. In the wooded areas, conifers such as fir, larch and pine dominate, but particularly at the eastern end there are large forests of beech.

Like the flowers, animals have to be capable of surviving extreme

Edelweiss, with its star-like petals, is the symbol of the German and Austrian Alpine Clubs

conditions, living on slim pickings. Previous visitors to the Alps will be familiar with the whistling warnings issued by a marmot leader who, spotting or smelling an interloper, tells his colony of fat meerkat-like creatures to get back into their rocky burrows. Less common and generally seen only in the distance are the chamois and ibex. Both in the past have been hunted to near extinction and both are happily in recovery. Much rarer, and warning signs suggest they should be avoided, are the brown bears whose meagre numbers are also on the increase.

The Alps are not a particularly rich habitat for birds. Most common is the alpine chough, a small hyperactive crow specifically adapted for high altitude. If you see a raptor it is likely to be a common buzzard, although there are also honey buzzards around. There are about 350 pairs of golden eagles in the Austrian Alps so if you're lucky you might see one of them.

In addition to coping with the alpine conditions, plants and animals must also compete with agriculture and the annual cycle of transhumance, the summer grazing of sheep and cattle in the mountains. Particularly on the Austrian side of the border, but in Italy as well, the lifestyle associated with transhumance remains central to the cultural identity of people living in the mountains, and the return down the valley of sheep and cattle, which takes place in mid September, is a major event for locals and tourists alike.

HOW HARD IS THE WALK?

The Karnischer Höhenweg is a well-defined alpine hike. The Alps, 'the playground of Europe', are where adventure travel began, and there is nowhere in the world that gets close to matching their 'walking infrastructure'. This includes the accommodation, the paths themselves, the waymarking, and the ropes, cables and ladders placed to enable obstacles and exposed stretches to be navigated with a high level of confidence.

The amount of accommodation available means that a range of day lengths can be catered for. To complete the walk in 2 weeks, however, including some of the optional highlights, expect to be walking for 6–8 hours per day, carrying a pack of 6–7kg and climbing around 1000m a day.

There are some stretches of walking where a head for heights is needed and where you might find cables and even ladders to help with progress and provide additional reassurance. This means that a wide range of walkers can manage what would otherwise be challenging walking. The stretches requiring a head for heights can be avoided but it would mean missing some of the best parts of the walk. It should be stressed that unless you intend to attempt some via ferrata options (not included in this guide: see below), no specialist equipment is required. Providing you have the necessary head for heights and a sense of adventure, the Karnischer

THE KARNISCHER HÖHENWEG

Höhenweg is a good introduction to alpine walking.

This guide suggests variants to the main route, which usually involve climbing a local summit. None of these climbs require technical experience but, again, some of them involve steel cables and ladders. Each variant is accompanied by a brief description, including an indication of the degree of challenge associated with it.

Via ferrata options are not included in this guide, although there are lots of opportunities in the Carnic Alps for those with the expertise and equipment. This is where the sport of via ferrata was first developed, as climbers began to exploit the cables and routeways that were originally used for supplying troops on the top of the mountains.

The difference between walking in good and bad weather is enormous. On the Karnischer Höhenweg, it is generally easy to get down from the mountains, but cold weather, snow and poor visibility feature even in the middle of summer. Being a ridge walk, the Höhenweg is not a good place to be in an electrical storm. Weather forecasts should be carefully heeded and will be supplied to guests on request in the huts and hotels.

SELECTING AN ITINERARY

Halfway along the Karnischer Höhenweg the route divides into two, with alternative Austrian and Italian routes around Monte Cogliáns. The

Walking through trenchworks along the granite ridge approaching Reiterkarspitz (Stage 3)

route is described in 8 stages for the Austrian route and 10 for the Italian route; 8 days is the minimum amount of time needed to complete the whole route. Each stage is approximately a day's walking, but this should be regarded as a loose framework around which to plan your visit to the Carnic Alps rather than a strict menu. There is a lot to see and each stage has variants. The descriptions and information provided are designed to enable walkers to produce an itinerary that matches the amount of time they have available, their interest in World War I, and their willingness to climb some additional summits along the route.

SELECTING AN ITINERARY

The first decision is whether to take the Austrian or Italian route round Monte Coglians. The Italian route is recommended but it does involve a sustained stretch of cable-assisted walking. It is spectacular and the reward is a stay at the fabulous Rifugio Marinelli. If you wish to climb Monte Coglians, you will have to choose the Italian route.

The second decision is whether to walk through the World War I Open-air Museum. It is a fascinating journey, described as part of the Italian route, but it does in effect add 2 days to the itinerary. It is possible to take the Austrian route round Monte Coglians (the easier route) and walk through the museum but this again takes 10 days.

The third decision relates to the balance of time spent on the first two-thirds of the walk and the final third. If the first part of the walk holds more interest for you, consider dropping the final couple of days and heading down to the valley by ski lift at Nassfeld. This would allow you to take the Italian route round Monte Coglians, visit the World War I Open-air Museum and complete all the best walking in 8 days.

Incidentally, many will regard the first stage from Arnbach to Obstanserseehütte, at 8hr 45min, as too long, and indeed other guides split this stage into two, staying at the Sillianer Hütte on the first night. This makes for a dull first day, however, spent climbing up through pine to the main ridge. If 8hr 45min is felt to be too long, then consider taking one of the ski lift options. The stretch of walking from the Sillianer Hütte to the Obstanserseehütte is awesome and guarantees that the trip along the Karnischer Höhenweg starts with a bang rather than a whimper.

The route summary tables at the beginning of this guide provide information on timings and distance for each stage of the walk. Appendix A offers a full route breakdown, with a summary of accommodation options and intermediate timings, to help you plot your own itinerary.

The tables below suggest two alternative itineraries: an 8-day trek taking in the highlights of the Karnischer Höhenweg; and a more leisurely 12-day option.

On the Sentiero Spinotti (Stage 4A)

27

The Karnischer Höhenweg

Highlights of the Karnischer Höhenweg: 8-day trek

Day	Time	Distance (km)	Notes
Day 1: Arnbach to Obstanserseehütte	8hr 45min	18.3	Consider taking ski lift
Day 2: Obstanserseehütte to Porzehütte	7hr 30min	13	Climb Große Kinigat
Day 3: Porzehütte to Hochweißsteinhaus	8hr	17.8	
Day 4: Hochweißsteinhaus to Rifugio Marinelli	8hr 50min	19.9	
Day 5: Rifugio Marinelli to Plöckenpass, with Monte Coglians	7hr 15min	13.9	Return along route and climb Monte Coglians
Day 6: Plöckenpass to Casera Pramosio	7hr 15min	11.2	
Day 7: Casera Pramosio to Straniger Alm	6hr 15min	13.4	Climb Hoher Trieb and continue to Straniger Alm
Day 8: Straniger Alm to Tröpolach	6hr	14	Take the Millennium Express from Madritsche Ski Station down to Tröpolach for trains to Villach
Total	**approx. 60hr**	**121.5**	

More leisurely option: 12-day trek

Day	Time	Distance (km)	Notes
Day 1: Arnbach to Sillianer Hütte	4hr 30min	8.6	Consider taking ski lift
Day 2: Sillianer Hütte to Obstanserseehütte	4hr 15min	9.7	
Day 3: Obstanserseehütte to Porzehütte	6hr 30min	12.2	Consider staying at Standschützenhütte after 3hr 40min
Day 4: Porzehütte to Hochweißsteinhaus	8hr	17.8	

GETTING TO AND FROM THE ROUTE

Day	Time	Distance (km)	Notes
Day 5: Hochweißsteinhaus to Wolayerseehütte	6hr	14.7	
Day 6: Wolayerseehütte to Plöckenpass	5hr 15min	10.4	Take the Austrian route but head south at Plöckenhaus; or go via Rifugio Marinelli and consider climbing Monte Cogliàns
Day 7: Plöckenpass to Casera Pramosio	7hr 15min	11.2	
Day 8: Casera Pramosio to Straniger Alm	5hr	13.4	
Day 9: Straniger Alm to Nassfeld	6hr 20min	17	
Day 10: Nassfeld to Eggeralm	4hr	14.2	
Day 11: Eggeralm to Gasthaus Starhand	4hr 20min	15.8	
Day 12: Gasthaus Starhand to Arnoldstein	8hr 30min	28	
Total	**approx. 70hr**	**173**	

GETTING TO AND FROM THE ROUTE

How much time you need is also influenced by where in the world you live, but getting to and from the Karnischer Höhenweg, located as it is right in the middle of Europe, is relatively easy. Getting on and off the Höhenweg, both at each end and at various points along the route, is particularly convenient, and for much of the route you are never more than 3 hours' walk from a railway station. The valley to the north of the ridge, known as the Lesachtal at its western end and the Gailtal at its eastern end, has a train running along it from Kötschach-Mauthen to the mainline station at Villach.

International connections to the route are also good, and all the cities listed below have international airports. Of these, Munich, Vienna and Venice have the best international connections. Particularly convenient for Sillian are:
- Innsbruck – train journey involving just one change (4hr) or there is also a bus that is just as fast as the train

THE KARNISCHER HÖHENWEG

The small cemetery at Hochgränten Pass is the highest wartime cemetery in the Alps (Stage 1)

- Salzburg – train journey via Lienz (4hr 30min)
- Munich – train via Innsbruck (5hr 30min)
- Venice – where a bus via Cortina provides the best route (6hr)
- Ljubljana – train journey via Lienz (6hr)
- Vienna – train journey via Lienz (6hr 30min).

From Arnoldstein it is possible to get to:
- Ljubljana – train and bus (2hr 30min)
- Venice – train (once daily) (2hr 30min)
- Salzburg – train (3hr 50min)
- Vienna – train via Villach (5hr 30min)
- Munich – train via Villach (6hr)
- Innsbruck – train via Salzburg and Villach (6hr 20min).

WHEN TO GO

The persistence of winter snow and the likely arrival of new snow in the autumn determine the relatively short length of the walking season in the Alps – from early July through to the third week in September. The huts only open when the snow disappears and walkers start to turn up.

Although it varies from year to year, lingering snow in July is possible. Alpine thunderstorms are more frequent in July and August, whereas September is the most settled month. The peak season, coinciding with holidays, is August, so if you're not tied to the holiday season, timing a trip to make the best use of September makes a lot of sense. The only downside is that the alpine flowers will be past their best.

ACCOMMODATION AND FOOD

What makes the Alps in general and the Carnic Alps in particular especially accessible is the quality and extent of the accommodation. To walk the whole route involves staying in a mix of mountain huts and small hotels, although a strongly recommended option involves a couple of nights in farm stays, known in Italy as *agriturismo*. This interesting and varied 'package' forms a key part of the Karnischer Höhenweg experience.

The Karnischer Höhenweg is popular, so if you plan to walk it in August, it makes sense to book in advance. This is straightforward, although one of the huts (the Hochweißsteinhaus) asks for a deposit via bank transfer, which can be expensive outside the eurozone (although if you point this out, the requirement to pay a deposit may be dropped). If for whatever reason a booking can't be honoured, then ring and explain. The booking systems for the huts are currently developing rapidly, with online booking steadily becoming available. A list of accommodation, with contact details, is provided in Appendix B.

If booking by phone:
- To call an Austrian number from outside Austria, use the country

The Hochweißsteinhaus, nestled at the head of the Frohnbach Valley (Stage 3)

code (+43) followed by the area code minus any initial zero, then the rest of the number. To call from inside Austria, include the first zero of the area code. This applies to both landlines and mobile numbers.

- To call an Italian number from outside Italy, use the country code (+39) followed by the area code including the first zero. Area codes for Italian landlines always include an initial zero, whether you are calling from outside or inside Italy. Italian mobile codes begin with 3 (not with zero).

At least three nights on the Karnischer Höhenweg will be spent in mountain huts (*Hütte* in German, *rifugio* in Italian), of which there are hundreds scattered all over the Alps. If this is your first long-distance trip in the Alps, mountain huts may take some getting used to, but they are a key part of the alpine walking tradition and their origins date back to the explosion of alpine tourism in the 1890s. They were particularly popular in the German-speaking world, where they were promoted by the German Alpine Club (which at that time was a single club formed of affiliate clubs from Germany and German-speaking parts of the Austro-Hungarian Empire). The nearest non-alpine equivalent is a youth hostel. Accommodation is in open dormitories or slightly more expensive smaller rooms which, at busy times, will also be shared. The huts are very convivial (expect to meet the same people several times), never run out beer, and provide an

Austrian hut cuisine

opportunity for some sleep (depending on your room-mates) after a good day in the mountains.

As a minimum, three nights will be spent in huts on the Austrian side of the border, where German-style food is provided. Similar food is provided in the small hotels and is best described as 'hearty' rather than fine dining. Standard fare includes soup (*Suppe*) with large dumplings – either *Leberknödel* (liver dumplings) or *Speckknödel* (ham dumplings); *Gulasch*, often served with dumplings (*Semmelknödel*); spaghetti bolognese; and, of course, large sausages (*Bratwurst*) served with bread, mustard and sauerkraut. Less common in the huts but available everywhere else in Austria is the Austrian equivalent of fish and chips, a type of schnitzel cordon bleu, consisting of white meat (veal, turkey, chicken or pork) wrapped around cheese, with a covering of breadcrumbs and deep fried. This is not the best place for vegetarians. Vegetarian food may be available, but (even if you give advance notice) don't expect the standard to be anything more than basic.

It sounds like a cliché but the food just across the border (at Wolayersee there is an Austrian hut and an Italian hut within 200 metres of each other) improves dramatically. The full range of rustic Italian food becomes available – antipasti, pasta and rich main courses – and there is suddenly a choice of wine. The Rifugio Marinelli is my favourite hut anywhere in the Alps and serves wonderful food (restaurant standard), with an emphasis on friendliness rather than efficiency.

The two farmhouse stays are also wonderful – one (the Straniger Alm) is in Austria and the other (Casera Pramosio) in Italy – and they both win awards for cheese. Although I preferred the Austrian cheese, the food in the Italian farmhouse was particularly good, especially the breakfast. (Be warned that at Casera Pramosio they speak no English, and apparently few Italians understand their local dialect. The staff at Rifugio Marinelli will help you if you want to book ahead.)

Mountain *Gasthof* or *Gasthaus* accommodation represents a very broad spectrum, ranging from small hotels or inns to something altogether more primitive – primitive even compared to the mountain huts.

BUDGET

A reasonable rule of thumb is to budget 50–60 euros a day, although this depends on what you choose to eat and drink rather than the type of accommodation. There is little difference between the cost of a small hotel and a mountain hut, although sleeping in large and sometimes noisier hut dormitories can be cheaper.

All the huts recommended are owned by the Austrian or Italian Alpine Clubs, so Club members get a discount. If you're British, the simplest option is to join the British section of the Austrian Alpine Club – the

THE KARNISCHER HÖHENWEG

fee includes insurance. (See contact details in Appendix C.)

WHAT TO TAKE

The golden rule is to take only what is needed. Weight is a key consideration and the greater the load, the bigger the strain on the body, particularly the knees. Weigh everything and restrict the total load (excluding water) to no more than 6kg.

When packing, prepare for wet and cold weather; snow, particularly above 2000m, is not unusual. In addition to good quality waterproofs, pack a fleece or a lightweight down jacket, a warm hat and gloves. If your gloves are precious, then a pair of old gloves to protect the hands on the cable stretches could also be packed.

Hopefully, the 'problem' will be the sun rather than cold and wet so make sure you have a brimmed hat, high factor sunscreen, lip salve and sunglasses. With any luck, the cold- and wet-weather gear will stay at the bottom of your rucksack, and shorts and T-shirts will be the order of the day. For emergencies, carry a head torch (also useful in the huts during 'lights out'), a whistle and a compact first aid kit.

For the huts, as well as personal toiletries, pack a lightweight towel, a sheet sleeping bag and earplugs. Outdoor shoes aren't allowed in huts; although indoor shoes are provided, you may still need to carry some sort of lightweight shoes for use in hotels and when travelling.

This guide describes food options for each day's walking. There is usually somewhere to stop for refreshments but emergency rations and snacks should be carried. Everyone will have their own emergency ration solution but a bar of chocolate hidden at the bottom of the rucksack (out of the sun and to avoid temptation) is mine. Walkers usually fill their water bottles in the huts, and there is no charge for this.

A comfortable rucksack is an essential item but it's more likely to be comfortable if the total load is only 6–7kg. It needs a waterproof cover. Stuff bags within the rucksack might also help; they hardly weigh anything and impose a bit of order when things are getting packed in the morning.

Footwear should also be light. Remember that 1kg on your feet is equivalent to 4kg on your back. Heavy boots, in particular, should be avoided. Many walkers (me included) have abandoned boots altogether for summer walking, opting for 'approach shoes' or fellrunning trainers instead. Lightweight footwear means feet stay cooler, skin is less likely to blister and you can walk further without getting tired.

ROUTEFINDING

The Karnischer Höhenweg is well waymarked and, providing the weather is reasonable, finding your

ROUTEFINDING

Excellent waymarks at Steinkarspitze (Stage 3)

way is easy. Generally the path follows route 403, a route defined both in terms of local signs and relevant paper maps. Signposts are positioned at each significant junction and pass, and between the signposts there are marks (red, white, red – the Austrian flag) painted on rocks or (when crossing a meadow) on poles.

GPS

Although most walkers now have a smartphone, many still don't use its GPS functionality, although GPS is the cheapest and most effective way of taking the stress out of navigation. A GPS tells you where you are and getting this right is usually the key navigational challenge. If you already have an Android or Apple smartphone, you can download a GPS app and buy the required digital maps. My recommended app is a product called Viewranger (www.viewranger.com), which has in its map store all the digital maps needed for the Karnischer Höhenweg.

In addition to a smartphone and a GPS app loaded with the right maps, you need GPX tracks of the route itself. These are available for free, stage by stage, on the Cicerone website: www.cicerone.co.uk/942/GPX.

The main GPS challenge is learning how to use it, so practice should be part of pre-trip preparations – don't leave it until you get to Austria. Smartphone GPS doesn't use 'data roaming' so you don't need to have that facility turned on. The battery on

THE KARNISCHER HÖHENWEG

the smartphone should be adequate for a day's walking, particularly if you remember to turn off any facilities that you're not using. (Phones permanently searching for a Wi-Fi connection consume a lot of energy.) If you are nervous about battery life, then take a supplementary battery and recharge the smartphone as needed.

Printed maps

Although GPS is becoming increasingly popular, some walkers will still want the additional security of paper maps (despite the extra weight) and printed maps will provide more context for the journey. Maps are best acquired in advance. The following Kompass maps (scale 1:50,000) are needed:
- No. 47: Lienzer Dolomiten, Lesachtal, Karnischer Höhenweg
- No. 60: Gailtaler Alpen, Karnische Alpen, Oberdrautal
- No. 64: Villacher Alpe, Unterdrautal.

In the UK, these maps are available from Stanfords (www.stanfords.co.uk) and The Map Shop (www.themapshop.co.uk): see Appendix C for full contact details.

SAFETY AND EMERGENCIES

In general, be prepared by carrying a basic first aid kit and knowing what to do in case of emergencies: see the 'Mountain Safety' page at the beginning of this guide. In the mountains, mobile phone coverage is patchy; but if you can get a connection, help should be available in English on the European emergency number 112.

It is essential to be adequately insured. Alpine club membership includes policy cover for high-altitude walking, and the British Mountaineering Council provides a range of policies to suit different mountaineering activities. Note that standard holiday insurance packages often don't include outdoor pursuits or helicopter rescue.

At the time of writing, UK residents carrying a European Health Insurance Card (EHIC) should be able to secure free health care, but this may be subject to change in the event of the UK leaving the European Union.

USING THIS GUIDE

Each stage in the guide begins with an information box giving basic data including distance, walking time, total ascent/descent and maximum altitude. A difficulty grading is also indicated for each stage:
- easy – essentially flat
- moderate – could involve physical exertion but with no exposed walking
- challenging – a head for heights required and could involve exposed sections.

The information box is followed by a brief introduction to give you a feel for the day's walking. Alternative schedules for each stage are then

Looking into the South Carnic Alps from Stage 3's beautiful ridge walk

described, drawing attention to options that should be considered in the event of bad weather and pointing out any more challenging stretches of walking.

There then follows a detailed description of the route, including information about accommodation and other facilities. All the stages include route variants (apart from Stage 8, although it does still include an optional ascent), which are included on the maps for each stage and described briefly in the text.

The route descriptions should be read in conjunction with the route maps, which are produced at 1:50,000. These show all the features highlighted in **bold** in the route descriptions. The maps and route descriptions, used in conjunction with printed maps or GPS information, should help you make sense of what you see on the ground.

Also provided are route profiles for each stage, showing the climbs involved and the anticipated time needed to get from point to point. Once in the mountains, it should be easy to see how your performance compares with the timings given and adapt the guide timings to your own pace.

Language

In this part of the world, places and geographical features on the Italian side of the border often have two names – a German name and an Italian name. Generally speaking, this

Multi-coloured rock face of Torkarspitze (Stage 3)

book uses the Italian name if the place or feature is in Italy and the German name if it's in Austria or on the border.

The letter 'ß' is often used in German instead of 'ss', for example Großglockner, Hochweißsteinhaus. It is pronounced as 'ss'. You may see the same place name spelt differently on signposts and maps, in books and other literature, sometimes with 'ss' and sometimes with 'ß', for example Nassfeld and Naßfeld.

THE ROUTE

Descending to the Oberer Stuckensee (Stage 2)

STAGE 1
Arnbach to Obstanserseehütte

Start	Alpenhotel Weitlanbrunn, Arnbach
Distance	18.3km
Ascent/Descent	1900m/550m
Difficulty	Challenging
Walking time	8hr 45min
Maximum altitude	2665m
Refreshments	Sillianer Hütte, just over halfway and reached after all the major climbing has been completed, is an excellent place to stop if lunch is not being carried. If you want to take food with you, you will need to go to Sillian as there are no shops in Arnbach.
Routefinding	Excellent waymarking: follow signs marked 403. Note that some maps show the route heading north around Hollbrucker Spitze, whereas our route follows the signs on the ground and heads south.

Stage 1 is a walk of two halves. The first involves a relatively dull walk up through conifers to the Sillianer Hütte, while the second, from the Sillianer Hütte to the Obstanserseehütte, provides a dramatic introduction to classic Karnischer Höhenweg ridge walking. Although the walk up to the Sillianer Hütte involves some 1200m of climb, most of it is along a nicely graded track and provides a good chance to warm up for the challenges ahead. Information boards placed at intervals along the route describe various features of mountain life and geology, offering some compensation for the lack of views.

The walk from Sillianer Hütte to Obstanserseehütte is fabulous, with great views south into the Sesto Dolomites and north into the Hohe Tauern. It is particularly rich in World War I earthworks and other wartime remains. It also involves some tough walking, including scrambling and some exposed paths.

STAGE 1 – ARNBACH TO OBSTANSERSEEHÜTTE

ALTERNATIVE SCHEDULES

If time is not a constraint, and 8hr 45min is felt to be too long for a first day (not an unreasonable conclusion!), then the obvious alternative schedule, favoured by many Germans and Austrians, involves staying at the Sillianer Hütte and dividing the stage into two almost equal parts. This allows time to climb Hochgruben (2537m), Hornischegg (2546m) and Hollbrucker Spitze (2580m). In addition, instead of taking the direct route to the Obstanserseehütte, you could continue further round the ridge to the Sella Frugnoni before heading down to the hut. If all these variants are taken, allow about 6hr to get from the Sillianer Hütte to the Obstanserseehütte rather than 4hr 15min.

If time is a constraint, or if you feel life is too short to waste it climbing through pine trees, then much of the first part of the walk can be avoided by taking a ski lift up from Sesto on the southern side of the ridge or from Versciaco on its northern side. There is plenty of accommodation in both places as well as good bus connections.

The alternative routes and their impact on timings are described briefly below, alongside the main route description.

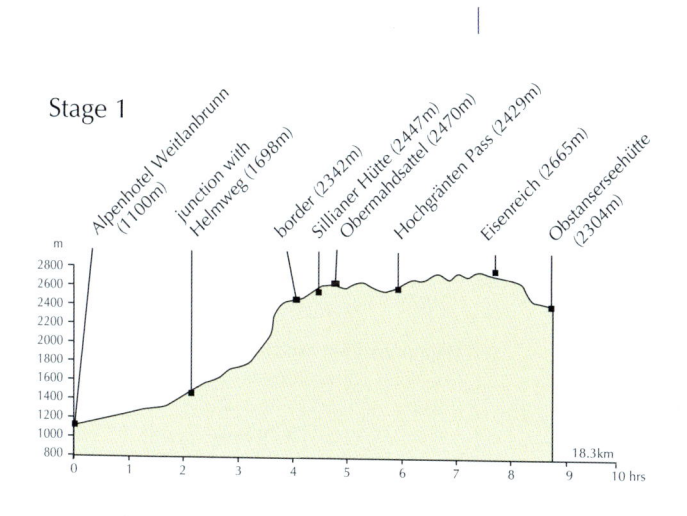

The Karnischer Höhenweg

Alternative start: Helmweg variant – moderate

The Helmweg provides an alternative way of joining the Karnischer Höhenweg, and is particularly relevant if you're staying in Sillian and prefer to follow a path up through the trees rather than a dirt road. It's slightly more direct than the route from Arnbach and consequently steeper.

From Sillian, join the Helmweg by crossing the most westerly of three bridges over the River Drau. On the Kompass maps, the route is marked as 473 and E10. Follow the route up to a junction where it merges with the 403.

Alternative start: Ski lift variants – moderate

This variant is relevant if you have stayed at Sesto or Versciaco and caught the ski lift up to the ridge. To join the Karnischer Höhenweg, leave the ski lift station and **Helm Restaurant** and head east along a dirt road following signs to the Italian hut **Rifugio Gallo Cedrone** (2150m).

From the hut, there are two options, both of which are well waymarked. For the more scenic but longer option, follow route 4. This goes via the summit of **Helm** (2434m), from where there are excellent 360-degree views, and then follows the ridge to join up with the Karnischer Höhenweg at the **pass and border**. The other option, avoiding the summit, takes a more direct route, again joining up with the Karnischer Höhenweg at the pass and border.

From the top of the ski lift, it takes about 2hr to get to the Sillianer Hütte if you visit Helm summit and 90min if you don't.

Main route from Arnbach

The walk starts from the Alpenhotel Weitlanbrunn (1100m), situated in trees to the south of the village of Arnbach. If arriving from Sillian along the main road, take the first left after the main road crosses the river, head south to a fork, turn right and continue past the fire station to the hotel.

STAGE 1 – ARNBACH TO OBSTANSERSEEHÜTTE

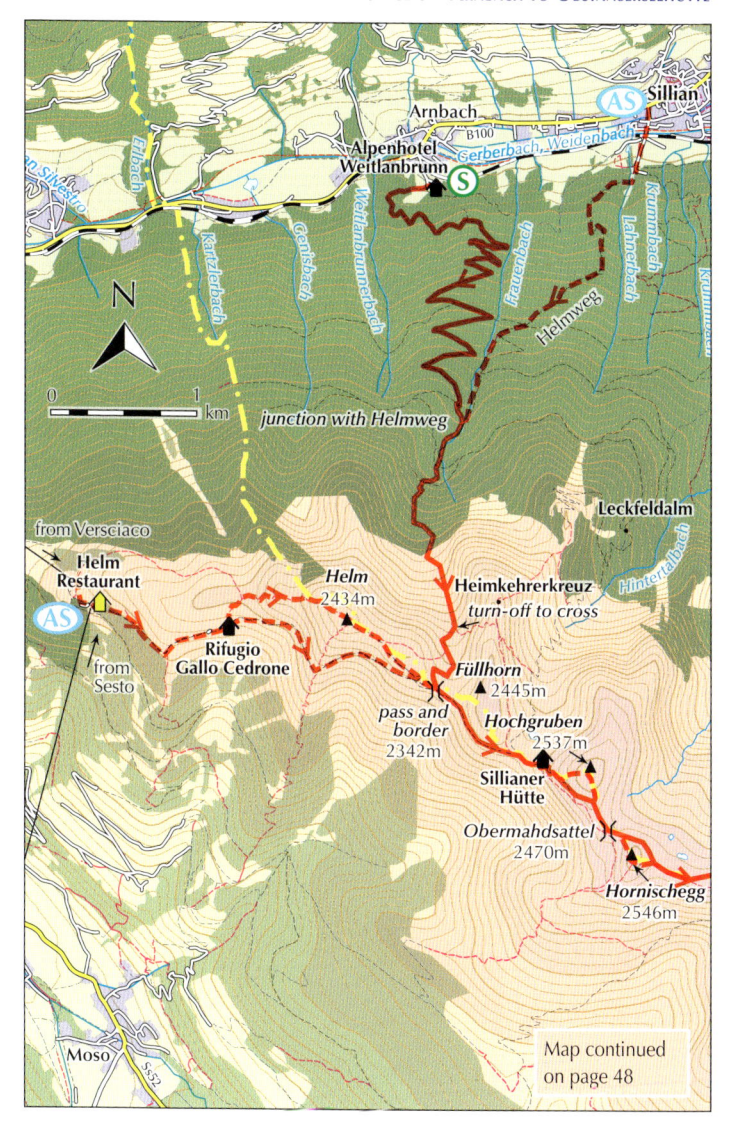

THE KARNISCHER HÖHENWEG

The **Alpenhotel Weitlanbrunn** (tel +43 (0)4842 6655 www.weitlanbrunnosttirol.com), perfectly located for the start of the walk, is a classic ski resort hotel providing four-star accommodation on half-board basis. It's a very comfortable hotel and if you want to eat a lot of food (buffet style) then it's a good option. There are, however, cheaper places to stay in Sillian. For a less perfectly located option, consider the **Hotel Schwarzer Adler** (mob +43 (0)650 5307229).

From the south-west corner of the hotel car park, follow a switchbacking dirt road (signed 'Karnischer Höhenweg 403') through towering pine up the side of the valley. After 50min and a climb of 350m, the dirt

Climbing up through the forest on the 403

STAGE 1 – ARNBACH TO OBSTANSERSEEHÜTTE

road reaches a junction. Ignore the turn-off to the Forcher Kaser and continue along the 403.

After following the dirt road for another 25min, including a further climb of 170m, a sign tells you that the Sillianer Hütte is 2hr 30min away and directs you left off the road along a path. After 100 metres or so along the path, it starts to follow a small stream and then reaches a **junction with the Helmweg** (1698m), an alternative route up from Sillian. Here, the two paths merge into one.

From the junction of the two paths, continue up to another junction where a path heads to Leckfeldalm (the sign is on a tree). Bear right here and follow the 403 past a wooden trough with drinking water. With the trees getting sparser and smaller, continue up the path, which eventually emerges into an open bowl above the tree line. The ridge should now be in sight. Above and to the left, a cross, the **Heimkehrerkreuz**, should be visible. ▶ Ignore the **turn-off to the cross**, and 10min later ignore another turn-off heading south-west to Helm. Continue across open grassy terrain up to the **pass and border** (2342m) between Austria and Italy.

> The Heimkehrerkreuz was constructed by World War II combatants to give thanks for their safe return.

THE BORDER

The border between Austria and Italy runs along the ridge and is marked by small rectangular stone plinths embossed '1921'. These plinths will become a familiar sight as you journey east along the Karnischer Höhenweg. The history of the two countries is closely related; both were formed as the Austrian Empire and subsequently the Austro-Hungarian Empire declined and collapsed.

Italian nationalism – along with nationalism across Europe – became a major force in the first half of the 19th century. In 1861 most of the states of the peninsula were united under King Victor Emmanuel II of the House of Savoy, which ruled over Piedmont. This followed a secret deal, known as the Plombières Agreement, between France (Napoleon III) and Piedmont (Cavour), whereby France agreed to support Piedmont's insurrections in the states of northern Italy that were ruled by the Austrian Empire. The border through the Carnic Alps was established five years later, in 1866, when the

The Karnischer Höhenweg

Austrian Empire ceded Veneto and western Friuli to Italy after being defeated in the Austro-Prussian War and the Third Italian War of Independence.

For Italy, 1866 was not the end of nationalist aspirations. Italy wanted the border moved north into Trento and east around Trieste, despite each of these areas containing only a minority of Italian speakers. Before World War I, Italy was notionally part of the Triple Alliance with Germany and the Austro-Hungarian Empire but didn't join in when fighting started in 1914. Instead, and after another secret agreement, Italy entered the war in 1915 on the side of the Triple Entente. The secret deal agreed that Italy would be rewarded with Trento and Trieste.

After three years of fighting, the Austro-Hungarian Empire effectively collapsed in the last few days of the war and new borders were established by the Treaty of Saint-Germain-en-Laye between the victorious Allies and the short-lived German–Austrian Republic. This concluded the formal dissolution of the empire and established Austria.

Austria's border with Italy through the Carnic Alps mostly follows the one established in 1866; but at the western end, instead of heading south around the Dolomites, it heads west-north-west along the alpine watershed to Switzerland. At the eastern end, instead of turning south to the Adriatic near Nassfeld, it continues east to Thörl-Maglern.

From the **pass**, head south-east to join a dirt road and follow it, climbing, around the south flank of a small summit, the Füllhorn (2445m). The **Sillianer Hütte** (2447m) should then come into view.

The **Sillianer Hütte** (mob +43 (0)664 5323802 www.alpenverein.at/sillianerhuette) is an Austrian hut in an absolutely stunning location. Positioned at the end of the Carnic ridge, it provides wonderful views west-north-west into Austria and south into Italy. You should be able to work out where the Tre Cime di Lavaredo (Drei Zinnen) are, although from this angle don't expect to see all three peaks. The hut is particularly accessible so it can be busy, especially at weekends, for much of the day. There are 40 dormitory beds and some smaller rooms.

Leaving Sillianer Hütte

THE SESTO DOLOMITES

Early morning view of the Sesto Dolomites

The Sesto Dolomites (Sexten in German) are arguably the most beautiful part of the world's most beautiful range of mountains, and looking at them from across the deep Val Pusteria is one of the best ways to see them. Although it's hard to spot the most famous summits, the Tre Cime di Lavaredo (Drei Zinnen), from the north-east, the great wall of mountains is presented to its best effect. The Sesto Dolomites are a climber's paradise, with hundreds of different routes, over 50 of which are on the Tre Cime alone. The highest summit, close to the Tre Cime, is the Punta dei Tre Scarperi (3152m), and there are two other summits over 3000m.

The World War I front line went through the Sesto Dolomites. There is a war museum maintained by the Dolomitenfreunde (Friends of the Dolomites) at Monte Piana, where mining in the mountain meant that one front line was immediately above the other.

The **summits of the western Carnic ridge** from Helm through to Pfannspitze (climbed at the beginning of Stage 2) are geologically similar, consisting of ancient volcanic shale and gneiss – the same rocks as are found in the central core of the Alps to the north.

If you choose to break this stage by staying at the Sillianer Hütte, you should have time to take in the little summits of Hochgruben (2537m), Hornischegg (2546m) and Hollbrucker Spitze (2580m) on the way to the Obstanserseehütte. Of the three, Hollbrucker is the steepest and

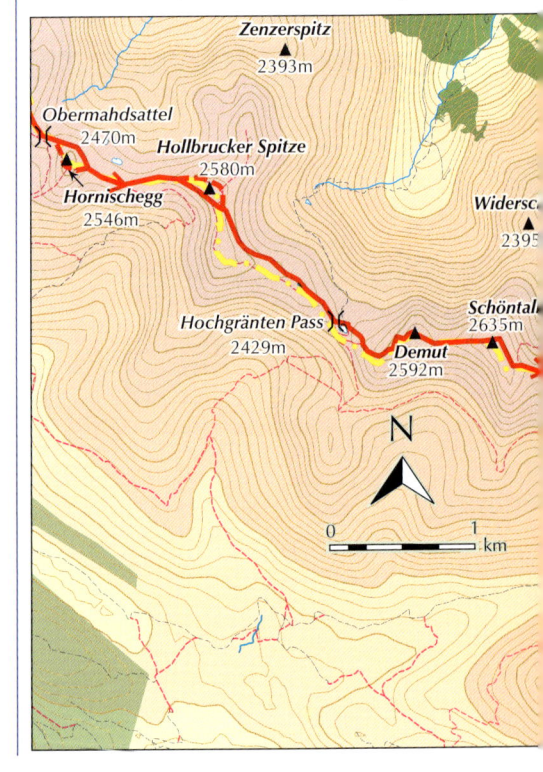

STAGE 1 – ARNBACH TO OBSTANSERSEEHÜTTE

Hornischegg has the best wartime remains, including some well-preserved trenchworks.

From the Sillianer Hütte, continue east along a well-defined path skirting round the southern side of **Hochgruben**. ▶ The path around Hochgruben ascends slightly, passing near some old military barracks that are probably connected with an old border post rather than with World War I. After 600 metres and a small descent, the path reaches a pass, the **Obermahdsattel** (2470m).

From the pass, continue along a fairly level path around the northern flank of **Hornischegg**. ▶ Continue

For the easy climb over Hochgruben, join a path before the military barracks and rejoin the main route at the Obermahdsattel.

To climb Hornischegg, turn right just beyond the pass and rejoin the main route about 600 metres from where you turned off.

THE KARNISCHER HÖHENWEG

east; after 600 metres, you pass the junction with the path descending from Hornischegg. About 10min later (there are two small lakes below to the north), the route reaches another junction and presents the option of climbing **Hollbrucker Spitze** (2580m), another fortified summit with well-preserved fortifications.

If you are not going over Hollbrucker Spitze, turn right. (Some maps show the main route heading around the north side of Hollbrucker, but our route follows the sign on the ground, which points south.) Follow an exposed path below the summit to where, after 400 metres, it reaches a junction with the return path from the summit. Continue east, descending a lovely path (trenches on one side) to a little lake, the Hochgräntensee, and the **Hochgränten Pass** (2429m). ◀

The Hochgränten Pass is much favoured by sheep, probably Italian sheep. If the weather is warm, the lake is a good place for a high-altitude swim.

THE WAR IN THE MOUNTAINS

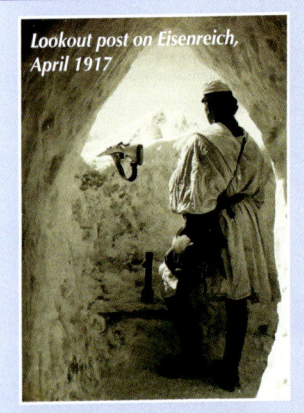

Lookout post on Eisenreich, April 1917

The remains of four Austro-Hungarian soldiers, killed in the first months of the war, lie in the small cemetery at Hochgränten Pass (the highest wartime cemetery in the Alps) – just a tiny proportion of the casualties from a truly gruesome conflict. In three years of fighting, Italy suffered over a million casualties, even more than the UK lost in four years, with deaths from disease, cold and malnutrition exceeding comparable British casualties by a factor of five.

At the outbreak of war, in May 1915, neither Italy nor Austria–Hungary was well prepared, and the latter had already lost nearly half a million men fighting on other fronts. However, Austria–Hungary had the advantage of limited objectives, prepared mountaintop defensive positions, and far more machine guns.

The Italians wanted 'Trieste and Trento', and after it became clear that the Austro-Hungarians could not be shifted from positions along the Carnic front, attention shifted decisively to the east, with Trieste the objective. The

STAGE 1 – ARNBACH TO OBSTANSERSEEHÜTTE

Isonzo front, where the Italians initiated 11 major campaigns without ever achieving a decisive breakthrough, was the bloodiest. The 12th Battle of Isonzo, also known as the Battle of Caporreto, was an Austro-Hungarian–German initiative, and with the help of German troops and extensive use of poisonous gas, a decisive breakthrough was achieved in November 1917. Italian troops on the Carnic front, in danger of being outflanked, had to withdraw, with a new front eventually being formed out of the mountains along the banks of the River Piave.

The Austro-Hungarians attempted one more offensive in June 1918 (coordinating with the German offensive on the Western front) but this failed. The final Italian attack, the Battle of Vittorio Veneto, started on 24 October and finished on 3 November, securing the dissolution of the Austro-Hungarian Empire and contributing to the end of the war two weeks later.

The position of the front line until 1917 in general terms corresponds to the border pre-1914. In the west, it ran from the Swiss border south and around what is now South Tyrol and then north-east through the Dolomites (Marmolada was heavily contested) to the Carnic Alps. It then followed the main ridge of the Carnic Alps, turning south-east near Trogkofel and down to the Adriatic.

The path runs close to the lake and wartime cemetery at Hochgränten

THE KARNISCHER HÖHENWEG

THE LIENZ DOLOMITES AND THE HOHE TAUERN

On the northern side of the Carnic ridge, the Lienz Dolomites and the Hohe Tauern should now be visible. Although the Lienz Dolomites share, on a smaller scale, a similar profile to the Sesto Dolomites to the south, they are not considered to be part of the Dolomites. Sandwiched between the Drau and Gail valleys, they are actually part of the small range of mountains known as the Gailtal Alps.

To the north of the Drau valley, and with a series of distinct snow-covered peaks and glaciers, are the Hohe Tauern group of mountains. Running west to east, and part of the central core of the Alps, they are Austria's most significant range of mountains. They include (directly north) the Großglockner (3798m), Austria's highest mountain and the highest in the Alps east of the Brenner Pass.

The stretch from Demut to Schöntalhöhe is the most challenging part of the stage, steep and exposed in places, with some scrambling. In one place, a short bridge has been built using rails to straddle a gap in the path.

From the Hochgränten Pass, follow an engineered path on a switchback route for 150 metres up the west face of **Demut** (2592m) and head round the summit on its northern side. Follow a gently descending path across a saddle before climbing again and embarking on what is at times a challenging northern circumvention of **Schöntalhöhe** (2635m).

> **World War I remains** are everywhere. Holes chiselled into the side of the mountain, rotting floors and roofing materials, and more personal artefacts, including food tins and remnants of clothes, bear witness to the troops who sheltered here.

The saddle between Schöntalhöhe and the next summit, Eisenreich (2665m), is 1.3km long and the path much easier than the previous stretch. Still sticking to the northern side of the ridge, the path goes close to but doesn't quite reach the summit of **Eisenreich**. From here, follow the path, now descending gently, for 900 metres

STAGE 2

*Obstanserseehütte to
Porzehütte*

Start	Obstanserseehütte
Distance	12.2km
Ascent/Descent	740m/110m
Difficulty	Challenging
Walking time	6hr 30min
Maximum altitude	2678m
Refreshments	Standschützenhütte is a quirky little hut and should be visited even if refreshments are not needed.
Routefinding	Well marked throughout. The entire route after the 2587m junction just before Pfannspitze is the 403; the bad weather variant is also marked 403.

This is another brilliant walk, with the first stretch, to the Standschützenhütte, particularly wonderful. The walk is described as challenging because of exposed stretches on the ascent and descent of Pfannspitze (2678m) and the 500-metre traverse across a steep bank of scree immediately below Große Kinigat (2689m). These stretches can be avoided but the scenic sacrifice is massive.

The best view of the day is on the ridge approaching Pfannspitze. From here, in good weather, it's possible to look east along the main ridge and see the big limestone summits Große Kinigat, Porze (2599m), Monte Peralba (2694m) and the highest mountain on the Carnic ridge, Monte Coglians (2789m). Pfannspitze is the highest peak you have to climb to complete the Karnischer Höhenweg (other peaks are optional) and the views from the top are excellent.

Apart from the stretch either side of Pfannspitze, the route does not follow the border but runs to the south of it, crosses it, and then runs to its north. Wartime remains, therefore, are not as extensive as they were on the first stage.

THE KARNISCHER HÖHENWEG

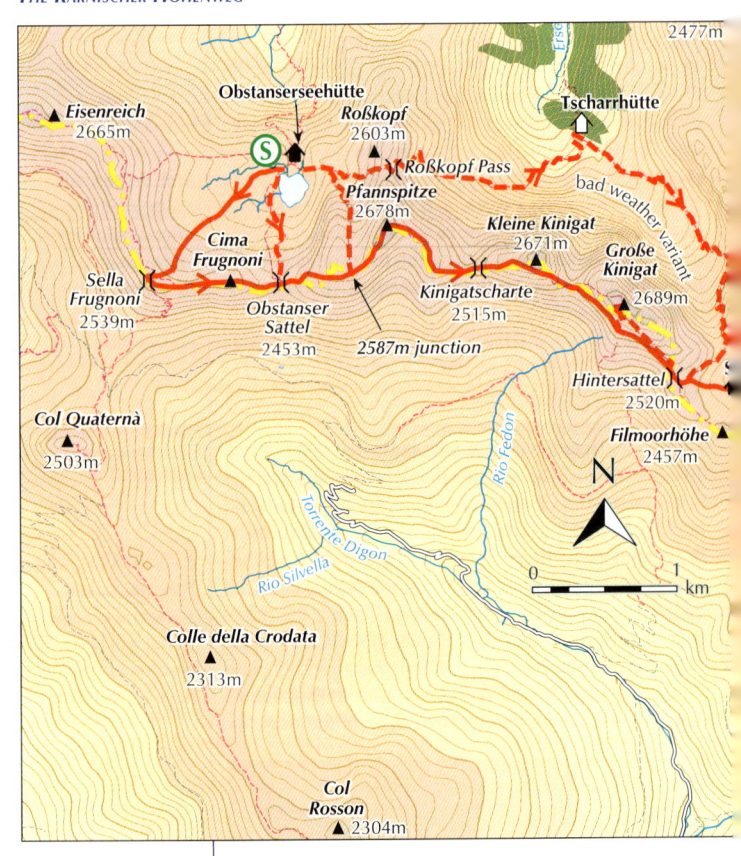

> The views east from here along the Carnic ridge are excellent. The cross at the top of Pfannspitze should be clearly visible.

500 metres where, after climbing about 100m, the route reaches the **2587m junction** with the second shortcut (the 403) from the Obstanserseehütte.

From the 2587m junction, the two shortcuts and the main route are now as one. This section of the route stays on the Austrian side of the border, swinging north and following an increasingly steep and exposed path up on the western side of a ridge, heading for the summit of **Pfannspitze** (2678m). ◄

STAGE 2

*Obstanserseehütte to
Porzehütte*

Start	Obstanserseehütte
Distance	12.2km
Ascent/Descent	740m/110m
Difficulty	Challenging
Walking time	6hr 30min
Maximum altitude	2678m
Refreshments	Standschützenhütte is a quirky little hut and should be visited even if refreshments are not needed.
Routefinding	Well marked throughout. The entire route after the 2587m junction just before Pfannspitze is the 403; the bad weather variant is also marked 403.

This is another brilliant walk, with the first stretch, to the Standschützenhütte, particularly wonderful. The walk is described as challenging because of exposed stretches on the ascent and descent of Pfannspitze (2678m) and the 500-metre traverse across a steep bank of scree immediately below Große Kinigat (2689m). These stretches can be avoided but the scenic sacrifice is massive.

The best view of the day is on the ridge approaching Pfannspitze. From here, in good weather, it's possible to look east along the main ridge and see the big limestone summits Große Kinigat, Porze (2599m), Monte Peralba (2694m) and the highest mountain on the Carnic ridge, Monte Coglians (2789m). Pfannspitze is the highest peak you have to climb to complete the Karnischer Höhenweg (other peaks are optional) and the views from the top are excellent.

Apart from the stretch either side of Pfannspitze, the route does not follow the border but runs to the south of it, crosses it, and then runs to its north. Wartime remains, therefore, are not as extensive as they were on the first stage.

ALTERNATIVE SCHEDULES

If the weather is bad, an alternative northern route around Große Kinigat should be considered. The original version of the Karnischer Höhenweg followed this and it is marked as such on older maps.

There are two attractive climbs along the route: Große Kinigat and Porze. Große Kinigat is the easiest and only adds 1hr to the schedule, whereas Porze takes 3hr so climbing it involves either splitting the stage and staying at the Standschützenhütte or staying for an extra night at the Porzehütte.

If both climbs are excluded, Stage 2 takes about 6hr 30min. This assumes that the most scenic but indirect route south-west to the ridge from the Obstanserseehütte is followed. There are also two shortcuts to the ridge, potentially reducing the time by about 1hr.

> **Bad weather variant via the original Karnischer Höhenweg – moderate**
> Head east from the Obstanserseehütte and follow a steep zigzagging path (the 403) up to the **Roßkopf Pass** (Roßkopftörl) and down the other side. Continue with the path, still marked 403, down into the Erschbaumer Valley to a shelter (unmanned hut), the **Tscharrhütte**. Turning south-east, join an old military road and climb up to the **Hintersattel**, rejoining the main route above the **Standschützenhütte**. In total, this variant takes about 3hr 30min.

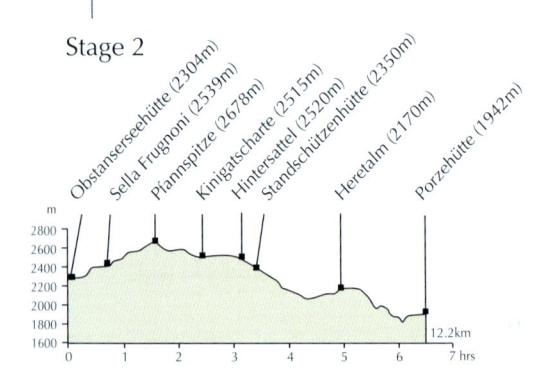

Stage 2 – Obstanserseehütte to Porzehütte

Shortcuts to the main ridge route – moderate

There are two shortcuts up to the ridge from the Obstanserseehütte. The first follows route 5A and heads directly south, to the west of the bowl in which the lake lies. The second one heads east on the 403 and turns south along a rocky gully behind a ridge to the east of the bowl. ▶ Neither shortcut is difficult but early on sunny mornings both will be in shade. Both these routes mean that less time is spent on the main ridge and the front line, but they do save time, shortcut 403 being the quickest.

Route 5A rejoins the main route at the **Obstanser Sattel**, and shortcut 403 rejoins it at an unnamed **2587m junction**.

Both the second shortcut and the original Karnischer Höhenweg (described above) are named 403.

Main route from the Obstanserseehütte

To follow the main route rather than the variants described above, leave the Obstanserseehütte and follow the path marked by red-and-white stones south-west across a boulder-strewn meadow towards the ridge. ▶ After 1.4km and a climb of nearly 200m, the path reaches the **Sella Frugnoni** (2539m) and turns east along the ridge. Follow a path sheltering on the south side of the ridge for 1km to the **Obstanser Sattel** (2453m) and a junction with route 5A, the first of the two shortcuts described above. Continue east along the northern flank of the ridge for

If you took the Sella Frugnoni variant at the end of Stage 1, you will have descended from the ridge via this path.

Signposts at Sella Frugnoni point the way

THE KARNISCHER HÖHENWEG

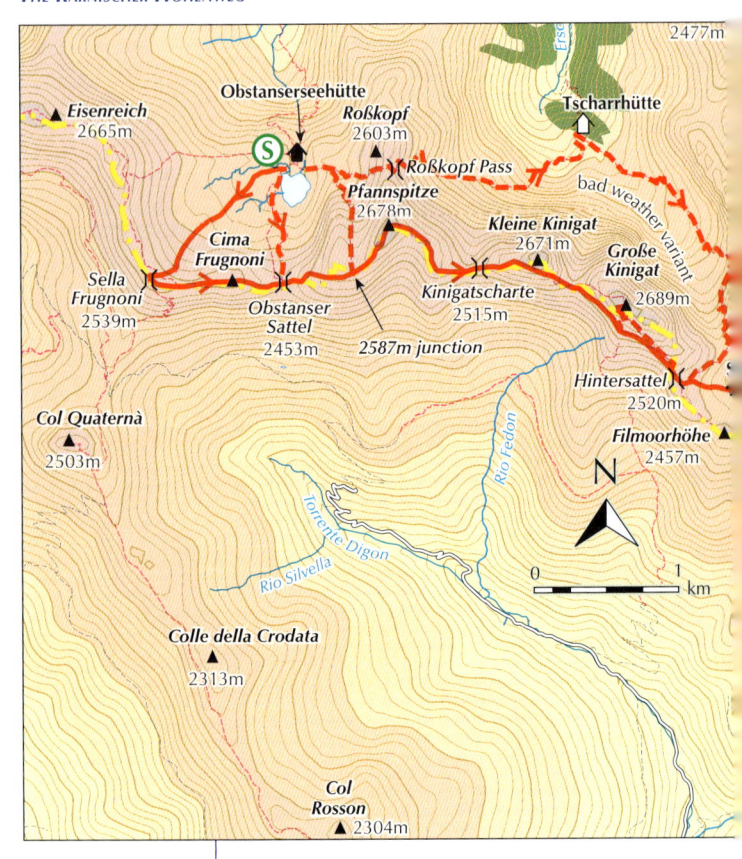

> The views east from here along the Carnic ridge are excellent. The cross at the top of Pfannspitze should be clearly visible.

500 metres where, after climbing about 100m, the route reaches the **2587m junction** with the second shortcut (the 403) from the Obstanserseehütte.

From the 2587m junction, the two shortcuts and the main route are now as one. This section of the route stays on the Austrian side of the border, swinging north and following an increasingly steep and exposed path up on the western side of a ridge, heading for the summit of **Pfannspitze** (2678m). ◄

STAGE 2 – OBSTANSERSEEHÜTTE TO PORZEHÜTTE

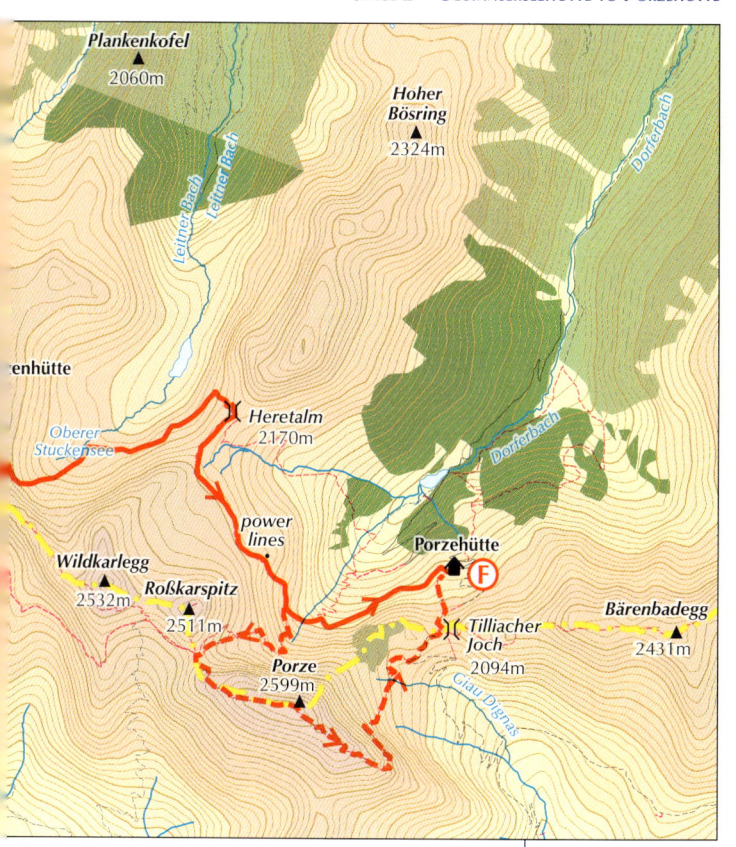

Pfannspitze is generally regarded as the first 'summit' on the Carnic ridge, because strictly speaking the earlier ones are not so much summits as high points on the ridge. It is the highest you have to climb on the Karnischer Höhenweg (the other peaks are all optional) and is the only 'summit' that isn't limestone.

THE KARNISCHER HÖHENWEG

Descending from Pfannspitze towards Kleine and Große Kinigat

Directly ahead are the twin summits of Kleine Kinigat (2671m) and Große Kinigat (2689m).

From Pfannspitze summit, the route descends steeply east (a little scrambling may be required) and follows a beautiful path immediately in the lee of a particularly narrow ridge and trenchworks. ◄ After an exciting ridge walk, follow a path navigating its way through some large boulders on the southern flank of **Kleine Kinigat** before reaching a pass, the **Kinigatscharte** (2515m).

From the pass, the route continues east, crossing a steep bank of scree, small rocks deposited from the huge cliffs on the south side of Große Kinigat. This is the first and most testing of a series of scree walks as

STAGE 2 – OBSTANSERSEEHÜTTE TO PORZEHÜTTE

the route moves into a limestone landscape. The clearly defined 900-metre path across the bank finishes at the **Hintersattel** pass (2520m). ▶

Optional ascent of Große Kinigat – challenging
This optional detour takes about 1hr and is well worth considering. About halfway across the scree before the Hintersattel, turn left at a junction onto a path up to **Große Kinigat**. It's a steep climb, with steel cables and wooden steps providing support at various times, so a head for heights and sure-footedness are required. On the descent, the route takes a slightly higher route back across the scree before rejoining the main route at the **Hintersattel**.

If the path halfway across the scree can't be found (it was poorly marked on my second trip across the scree in 2016), continue to the Hintersattel and make the climb by going back along the higher route.

From the Hintersattel, continue east to a junction and bear left. After 50 metres, pass the junction with the original Karnischer Höhenweg, the bad weather variant (described above). The **Standschützenhütte** (2350m), now about 200 metres away, should be clearly visible below. Continue east and down to the hut. ▶

> The **Standschützenhütte** (mob +43 (0)664 1127153 contact only by SMS www.alpenverein.at/filmoor standschuetzenhuette) is small and, for an Austrian Alpine Club hut, very informal, more like a student house than an alpine hut. It only has 14 places in a dormitory but has a lovely intimate dining room, providing a nice place to stop, rest and eat some cake or soup, particularly if it's cold outside.

Leaving the Standschützenhütte, head east and down through boulders onto an increasingly grassy and marshy hillside. The path, which swings around the head of the valley, can at times be a little difficult to follow but the destination, the lake – the **Oberer Stuckensee** (2032m) – should be easy to spot. Cross the stream that leads into it

---

Next to the route near the pass is a memorial to Walther Schaumann, halfway along the Peace Trail he founded.

The boggy hillside provides the ideal host for cotton grass.

Approaching the Heretalm

and continue walking for 1.6km to reach the lake. Staying on the right-hand side of the lake, the path then turns east at a junction with a road and starts its steady climb up to the next pass, the **Heretalm** (2170m).

If you're lucky, the sun shining on the two lakes, the Oberer and Unterer Stuckensee, will illuminate what is a pretty **alpine valley**. On the hillsides are little shepherds' huts, used for just a few weeks each year as the cattle or sheep don't stay this high for long.

Making your way through the cattle fences on the Heretalm, ignore the route (16A) heading to the Hoher Bösring and bear right, following a contouring path for almost 2km around the head of the next valley. Spoiling the view but providing a target that's easy to spot are some huge **power lines** (2181m). After passing underneath them, descend a steep gully with the help of steel cables before swinging east across a gully and underneath the north-facing cliffs of Porze. After 500 metres, you cross a junction. ◄ Unless the intention is to climb

This junction is the turn-off to the optional climb over Porze: see below.

STAGE 2 – OBSTANSERSEEHÜTTE TO PORZEHÜTTE

over Porze, ignore the junction. Continue down the track for 200 metres, cross the stream and start a small ascent on the other side of the valley. Ignore a left-hand turn after 200 metres and continue along a fairly even path for another 1.5km to the **Porzehütte** (1942m).

> Compared to the Obstanserseehütte, the **Porzehütte** (mob +43 (0)664 3256452 **www.alpenverein.at/ porzehuette**) feels a little old-fashioned. It's a reasonably big hut but all of its 64 places are in dormitories and tightly packed. As at the next hut (the Hochweißsteinhaus), you have to pay to get your phone recharged. It's a friendly hut, well managed, and serves good food that in good weather can be enjoyed outside on a sunny west-facing deck. The breakfast is a little expensive but involves an 'as much as you want to eat' buffet and no one seems to mind if you make your own sandwiches – really useful as there are no refreshments to be found on the next stage.

Optional climb over Porze – challenging

The climb over Porze presents an alternative way of getting to the Porzehütte, a diversion that involves about 700m of climb and will take an additional 3hr. ▶ The route includes ladders and steel cables and, although not technical, there is a risk, on the ladders, from falling rocks.

From the junction, follow a path climbing south-west up to the Porzescharte (2363m) and the main ridge. Turn east and follow the ridge to the summit of **Porze** (2599m). From the summit, head initially south-east on path 172 and follow signs down to a pass, the **Tilliacher Joch** (2094m), then head north and down to the **Porzehütte**.

Porze has extensive World War I remains and is significant for being the only mountain in the Carnic Alps to change hands during the fighting (captured by the Italians).

The Karnischer Höhenweg

STAGE 3
Porzehütte to Hochweißsteinhaus

Start	Porzehütte
Distance	17.8km
Ascent/Descent	1180m/1240m
Difficulty	Challenging
Walking time	8hr
Maximum altitude	2524m
Refreshments	None on the main route; Malga Antola on the bad weather route
Routefinding	Well waymarked: follow the 403

This is the best day on the Karnischer Höhenweg, a classic ridge walk with wonderful views – so good that it justifies a trip to Austria in its own right. It's been given a challenging status because it includes a couple of short stretches of cable-assisted walking, but unless the weather is really bad this walk should not be missed. Strongly recommended, particularly if the sun is shining, is a short and very easy climb up to Hochspitz (2583m), from where you can see right back into the heart of the Dolomites.

This stage involves another long stretch of granite ridge walking, where the route follows the watershed, border and front line, with an abundance of World War I earthworks.

ALTERNATIVE SCHEDULE

The bad weather alternative involves a 9hr route on the southern side of the ridge via Malga Antola. Nine hours in bad weather will be too much for most people, particularly given the disappointment of not doing the main ridge, but there is accommodation at Malga Antola, which can be reached in 5hr 30min. If you intend to walk this variant in a day, it's worth noting that it's a 500m climb over the Hochalpljoch pass.

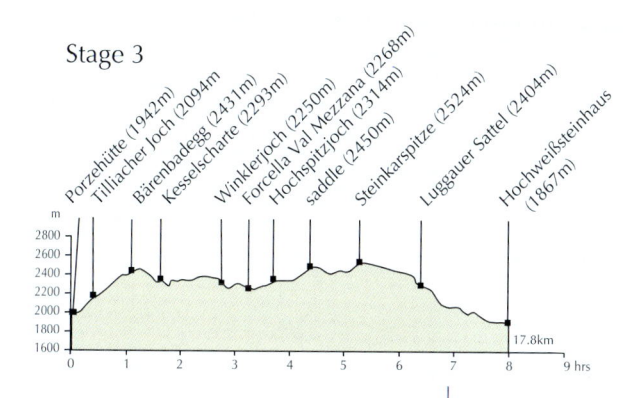

Stage 3 – Porzehütte to Hochweisssteinhaus

Stage 3

Porzehütte (1942m), Tilliacher Joch (2094m), Bärenbadegg (2431m), Kesselscharte (2293m), Winklerjoch (2250m), Forcella Val Mezzana (2268m), Hochspitzjoch (2314m) saddle (2450m), Steinkarspitze (2524m), Luggauer Sattel (2404m), Hochweißsteinhaus (1867m)

17.8km / 9 hrs

From the Porzehütte, follow the well-defined path (almost certainly in shade) south. The path takes the direct route up to the pass, the **Tilliacher Joch** (2094m), and is much steeper than the old military road, now a popular mountain bike route that switchbacks its way up to the same destination. The pass is where the route down from Porze (which you may have taken in Stage 2) rejoins the main trail; it is also the start of the bad weather alternative to the Hochweißsteinhaus.

Bad weather alternative to the Hochweißsteinhaus

The bad weather alternative follows the military road eastwards along the Malgenweg through a mix of south-facing alpine pastures (where large flocks of sheep typically graze) and forest.

Instead of turning east on the main route, stay on the dirt road and descend, switchbacking, from the pass. After about 3km, turn left at a junction and follow a contouring dirt road (403A) east for 10km, passing a farmstead, **Casera Campobon**, after 3km. Leave the dirt road at **Casera Chiastelin**, turn left and follow a path for another 4km to **Malga Antola**, where there is food and accommodation in an Italian farm (mob +39 348 3542460).

From Malga Antola, follow a road for about 2km to the next farmstead, **Malga Chivion**. Bear left at a

The Karnischer Höhenweg

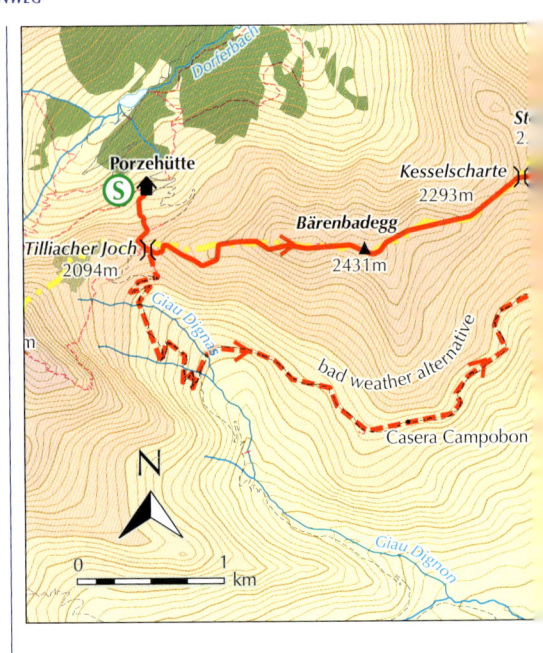

The buildings near the pass are old barracks associated with the border crossing rather than with World War I.

junction and continue for 800 metres to another junction. Bear left again and continue on an increasingly remote path on a steady climb up the **Hochalpljoch** pass (2281m). ◄ From the pass, head north and descend to the **Hochweißsteinhaus** (1867m).

Main route

From the junction at Tilliacher Joch, the main route leaves the military road and climbs east. Following a grassy path on the south of the ridge, climb steadily, gaining 300m over the next 2km. Staying on the grassy southern side of the ridge, there are some occasional stretches of exposed walking. If you can, avoid the temptation to climb up and look over the edge northwards; wait until the path passes just south of the little summit **Bärenbadegg** (2431m), which has the best views.

STAGE 3 – PORZEHÜTTE TO HOCHWEISSSTEINHAUS

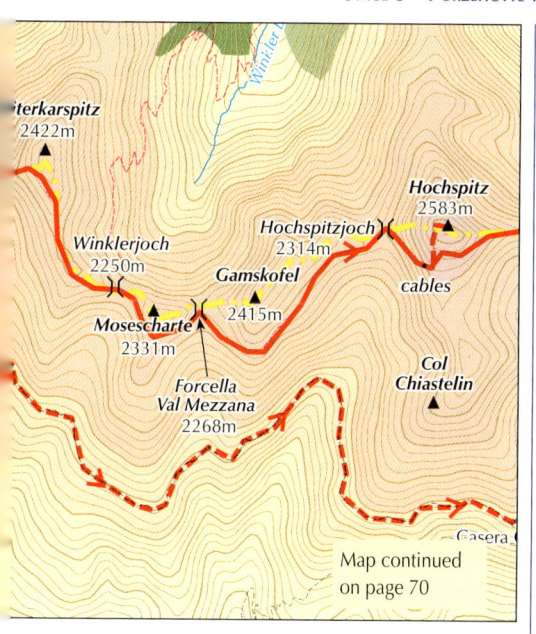

The **views from Bärenbadegg** are extensive. From the top of the ridge, looking north, the horizon is dominated by the snow-topped mountains and glaciers of the Hohe Tauern. Immediately below is the deep and very green east–west-running Lesachtal (Lesach Valley) and the village of Obertilliach.

Competing with views north are those to the west and back along the route. Immediately striking are the huge east-facing cliffs of Porze, hopefully illuminated by early morning sun. Behind Porze and to the south-west is the Crode dei Longerìn, which stands apart and in form is completely different from the other limestone summits on the main Carnic ridge. Its turrets and spires define it as dolomitic, like the great mass of the Dolomites which can be seen further across the valley to the south and south-west.

The Karnischer Höhenweg

Looking east and west along the ridge itself, it's worth noting that the limestone section that began at Kleine Kinigat on Stage 2 has given way to older Palaeozoic rocks. It's this, and the south-facing aspect of the slope, that produces a lovely grassy landscape much favoured by huge flocks of sheep.

Head east along a stunning ridge path down to a pass, the **Kesselscharte** (2293m). Ignoring the path (marked 19) that heads north over the pass, continue around the south side of the **Stollen** (2370m) along a gently descending path. After returning to the ridge, follow a beautiful path offering glimpses ahead, to the north-east, of the Lienz Dolomites. After 1km, the path reaches a junction offering a short detour up to **Reiterkarspitz** (2422m). Ignore

A perfect ridge walk near Reiterkarspitz

it (there are better detours to come) and follow the path as it swings south and down to a pass, the **Winklerjoch** (2250m). Ignore the junction with a path heading over the pass (marked 25) and follow a well-defined path east. For the next 2.6km, the walking is particularly easy and stays below the ridge underneath **Mosescharte** (although it approaches the ridge again near the **Forcella Val Mezzana**, 2268m), following a path that almost contours across gently sloping alpine meadows (hopefully sunlit) towards Hochspitz.

The most difficult section of this stage comes after reaching the pass, the **Hochspitzjoch** (2314m). From the pass, follow the path as it swings south-east and under the west face of Hochspitz. After about 400 metres, the path starts to climb steeply to a saddle. The path is almost hidden in a shady corner of the mountain, and for 50min or so **cables** are positioned to help with the climb to the top of the saddle (2450m).

Optional short climb to Hochspitz

The platform at the top of the cable-assisted climb is a good place to stop to take in the views, but it's well worth an extra, easy climb to the top of **Hochspitz** (2583m) for some of the best views on the Karnischer Höhenweg. The vantage point provides views of the Hohe Tauern and right into the heart of the Dolomites. Using the Crode dei Longerìn in the foreground as your marker, you should be able to see, firstly, to its left, Monte Pelmo, shaped like a huge citadel, and then to its east, and much further back, the Queen of the Dolomites herself, Marmolada, marked by a huge glacier.

The path to the summit, directly north from the saddle, is easy to follow. After visiting the summit, return the same way back down to the saddle.

From the saddle, continue along an easy path descending east, running just below the ridge. As the mountainside gets steeper and the ridge narrower, the path becomes more exposed and, after an indistinct pass, starts to ascend again. Once more there is a short stretch where cables

THE KARNISCHER HÖHENWEG

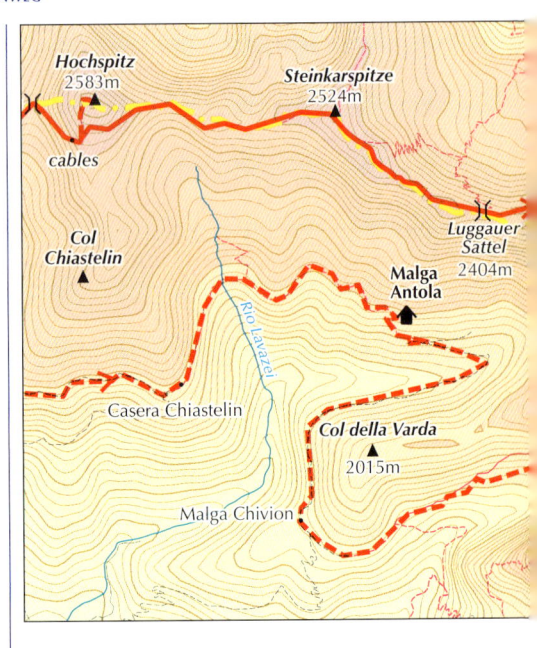

have been placed to assist the climb. The final approach to **Steinkarspitze** (2524m) is easy but open. At this height, even south facing, the slope is largely free of vegetation.

The sign on Steinkarspitze announces that the Hochweißsteinhaus is still 2hr 30min away. There is

Climbing Steinkarspitze

STAGE 3 – PORZEHÜTTE TO HOCHWEISSSTEINHAUS

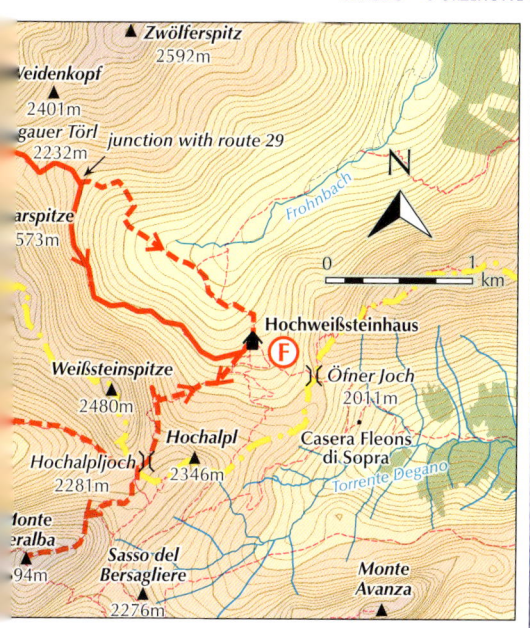

great walking still to come but the character of the route changes, mainly because it switches from the south to the north side of the ridge. If there is any late snow, it will still be in evidence, and the landscape and path feel less welcoming and more alien than during the first 5hr 30min of the stage.

After another 1.8km of steady descent through rocky terrain along a path that is narrow at times, running immediately below the ridge, the path reaches a pass, the **Luggauer Sattel** (2404m). From the pass, the path descends along an old military road and across a scree field underneath the huge and slightly intimidating cliffs of Torkarspitze (2573m). After 800m it reaches the grassy **Luggauer Törl** (2232m), the saddle between Torkarspitze and, to the north-east, Weidenkopf (2401m) and Zwölferspitz (2592m).

SUPPLYING THE FRONT LINE

Wartime ski patrol at Obere Luggauer Alm

This stretch of the route is a good place to contemplate the challenges involved in supplying the front line.

At the beginning of the war there was nothing in terms of transport infrastructure so, as the fighting descended into stalemate, both sides had to establish the means of supplying their troops. Initially, this relied on either animals (dogs, mules or ponies) or humans. The human cargo-carriers included Russian prisoners of war who had been captured before the fighting started on the Italian front. Over the two and a half years of mountain warfare, the infrastructure and technology developed rapidly, so that by the time the front moved, over 100 cable cars had been installed. Virtually all the technology currently used to sustain the skiing industry had its origins in World War I.

The area around the Luggauer Sattel is particularly rich in war remains. Here, unusually, the Austro-Hungarians found themselves facing an enemy looking down at them; their gun turrets carved out on the north-facing flank of Monte Peralba above are clearly visible. The Austro-Hungarians had to dig in, and the remnants of the huge road running just underneath the ridge are clearly visible.

STAGE 3 – PORZEHÜTTE TO HOCHWEISSSTEINHAUS

The multi-coloured north face of Torkarspitze presents a fabulous example of the complex **geology of the Carnic Alps**. The grey Silurian rock, the oldest type of rock, has sandwiched itself between younger Carboniferous (white) and Devonian limestone (pink), which are normally sequential in the geological time series.

Ignoring the path to the west and the path leading up to Torkarspitze, head east down into the valley. After 600 metres (and a descent of 200m) the path reaches a **junction with route 29**. This provides an alternative route (see below) to the Hochweißsteinhaus, which is now clearly visible on the other side of the valley.

For the official route, turn south and follow a well-defined contouring path around the head of the Frohnbach Valley for about 2.5km to where, emerging from the trees, it arrives at the **Hochweißsteinhaus** (1867m). Without significant ascent or descent, the route looks appealing, but looks can be deceptive. Positioned under the towering cliffs of the main ridge, deep crevasses have to be crossed and the route is subject to landslips. If you are feeling the effects of a long day, consider taking the alternative route (clearly visible from the junction) directly across the valley.

The **Hochweißsteinhaus** (mob +43 (0)676 7462886 www.alpenverein.at/hochweisssteinhaus) is similar to the Porzehütte in terms of age and facilities but somehow feels more intimate and friendly. Nestled at the top of the valley, it's another lovely hut in a beautiful location. There are 40 beds in dormitories and 12 beds in smaller rooms. As at the Porzehütte, you have to pay to get your phone recharged. Tap water in the hut is not drinkable, so most people use the little fountain outside to replenish their bottles.

To book accommodation at the Hochweißsteinhaus, you need to use the online booking system, which can be accessed via the hut's page on the Alpine Club website (see above). A deposit, payable by bank transfer, is required, which will involve a significant fee if you are booking from the UK; if you explain this, the requirement to pay a deposit may be dropped.

Alternative route to the Hochweißsteinhaus

Although this involves more descent and ascent than the main route, it is an easier path so takes the same amount of time (1hr 15min). From the junction, continue heading down the valley across a grassy hillside to where, after about 1.2km, the path hits a dirt road. Turn right onto the dirt road and follow it to the **Hochweißsteinhaus**.

Optional ascent of Monte Peralba – challenging

Monte Peralba (Hochweißstein, 2694m) is a popular climb, particularly from the Italian side, where climbers start from the Rifugio Calvi. From the Hochweißsteinhaus, the return trip takes about 4hr 30min. Although there is a steel-rope-assisted stretch of walking up through a gully, it is not a difficult ascent. ◄

> Famously, Monte Peralba was climbed in 1988 by Pope John Paul II, who made the ascent at the age of 68.

From the Hochweißsteinhaus, follow path 41 southeast, signposted to Rifugio Calvi and the Hochalpljoch, reaching the **Hochalpljoch** pass (2281m) in about 1hr 15min. Some 200 metres after the pass, turn right at a junction for the final climb to the summit of **Monte Peralba**, reached after about 2hr 45min. Return to the hut by the same route.

STAGE 4
Austrian route: Hochweißsteinhaus to Gasthof Valentinalm

Start	Hochweißsteinhaus
Distance	23.2km
Ascent/Descent	1180m/1820m
Difficulty	Moderate
Walking time	9hr
Maximum altitude	2138m
Refreshments	Wolayerseehütte reached after 6hr
Routefinding	Easy: follow the 403

Following three days of classic ridge walking, Stage 4 is a day of contrasts, mixing alpine mountain walking with a taste of the pastoral scenery that characterises the later stages of the walk. After an initial ridge, the route descends and ascends through a long remote valley, at the heart of which is our first farm dedicated to the summer production of cheese.

Crossing the front line and the border, the route then descends once again into another cattle-filled valley before making a pre-lunch, energy-sapping climb to the stunningly located Wolayerseehütte. Refreshments are needed because there is still some work to do as the path climbs through a shady valley up to yet another pass before starting its long descent to the Gasthof Valentinalm.

ALTERNATIVE SCHEDULES

There are two decisions to be made on this stage: firstly, how far to walk; and secondly, whether to walk on the Austrian or Italian side of the border after the Wolayerseehütte.

The first decision is straightforward. The Wolayerseehütte has recently been refurbished, is in a lovely location and, to avoid a long day, is a good place to stop. In addition, the Rifugio Lambertenghi Romanin, 300 metres to the south and just across the border, is another option if Italian food is preferred. Lots of Germans and Austrians finish their trip along the Karnischer Höhenweg at the Plöckenhaus, and they typically stop at the Wolayerseehütte, walk down to the pass the next day and catch a bus home from there.

The second decision – Austrian or Italian side – is more difficult. The Italian side, from the Wolayerseehütte to Rifugio Marinelli, is slightly shorter (2hr 30min) and more beautiful, finishing at what is the nicest hut on the whole of the Karnischer Höhenweg. Furthermore, if Monte Coglians (2789m), the highest mountain in the Carnic Alps, is to be climbed, the Italian route has to be taken. Unfortunately, its obvious attractions come at a price – it's a tough walk – and a significant proportion of the 280m climb after the Wolayerseehütte is cable-supported.

The weather will probably be the deciding factor. In good weather, reasonably fit walkers will arrive at the Wolayerseehütte by lunchtime. In good conditions and with the prospect of a brilliant afternoon's walking, the appeal of the Italian option will probably be overwhelming. If the weather is poor, however, walkers will probably stay where they are or continue to the Gasthof Valentinalm.

One additional factor to think about is the World War I Open-air Museum at the Plöckenpass, visited in Stage 5 or 5B. (Note that the Plöckenpass is on the border, not to be confused with the Plöckenhaus, a restaurant, which is in Austria about 1km north of the Plöckenpass.) The museum can be approached from either the Italian or the Austrian side. If, however, you intend to continue to the Zollnerseehütte from there, it is a marginally shorter day if approached from the Gasthof Valentinalm.

From the Hochweißsteinhaus, follow route 403 east along a path climbing steadily through meadows to a pass, the **Öfner Joch** (2011m), and over the border into Italy.

The Öfner Joch marks the entry into a stunning east–west-running valley, the **Val di Fleons**. Named after Monte Fleons/Raudenspitze (2507m), the first mountain on the ridge on its northern side, it is surrounded by a series of beautiful mountains. On the northern side, the mountains consist of dark volcanic rocks, whereas on the southern side, limestone predominates. Particularly striking is Monte

STAGE 4 – AUSTRIAN ROUTE: HOCHWEISSSTEINHAUS TO GASTHOF VALENTINALM

Chiadenis, whose classic citadel shape, formed from limestone, peeps over the ridge to the southwest. Monte Chiadenis was bitterly contested during World War I, and the via ferratas left from that conflict make it a favourite for climbers today.

Just to the north of the Öfner Joch is a statue depicting the good shepherd bringing home a lamb.

From the pass, continue east and down along a slightly boggy path past a pond. After 200 metres, the path traverses south and continues its descent to a junction with a path that has come down from Monte Chiadenis. Turning abruptly north, pass some long low buildings, the **Casera Fleons di Sopra** (1862m), which probably have some connection with the dairy farm Casera Fleons di Sotto in the valley bottom.

On some maps, a **cable car** links the Casera Fleons di Sopra and the Casera Fleons di Sotto. Its ancient cable, left on the ground, is crossed several times on the descent of the valley. Perhaps the cable is the remains of a World War I lift system and the buildings at the top were used to accommodate mules.

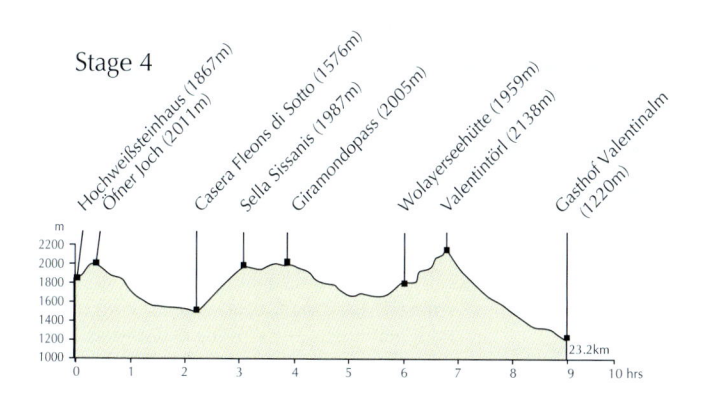

THE KARNISCHER HÖHENWEG

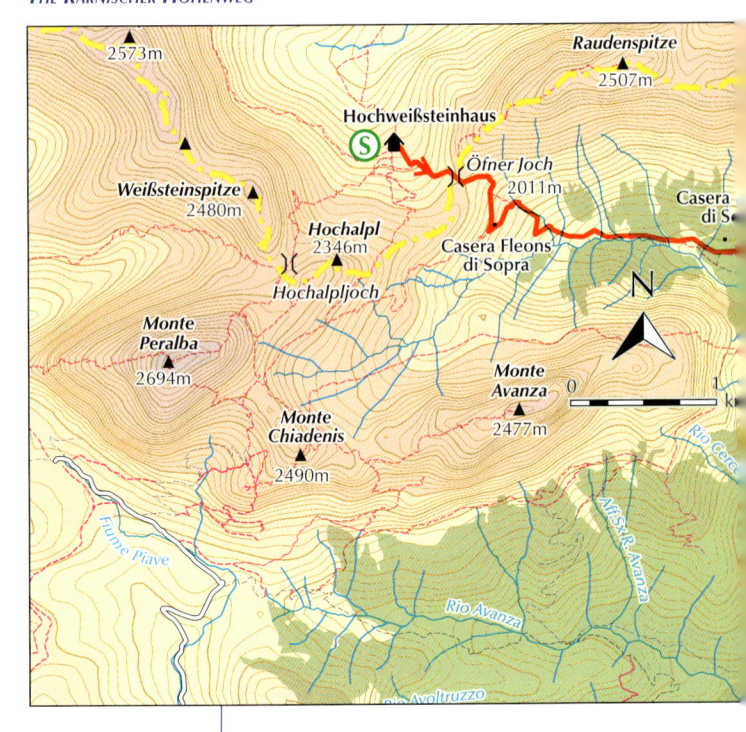

If you want to enjoy the authentic taste of the Val di Fleons, buy some of its cheese at the Casera Fleons di Sotto.

Continue past the buildings, following an increasingly well-defined dirt road down the valley into a forest of larch. After 1.6km, cross a stream that has washed away the road; just after this, bear left at a junction and join a path. Continue for another 500 metres to a large and interesting farmstead, the centrepiece of which is a splendid wooden farmhouse, the **Casera Fleons di Sotto** (1576m). It's difficult to tell whether the path passes close to the house or through the 'muddy' cattle yard just below it – I'd stick close to the farmhouse. ◄

From the farmstead, head east across a meadow and back into trees. After crossing two streams heading down from the north, pass a junction with the 142 and follow a steeply climbing path. After 600 metres from the

STAGE 4 – AUSTRIAN ROUTE: HOCHWEISSSTEINHAUS TO GASTHOF VALENTINALM

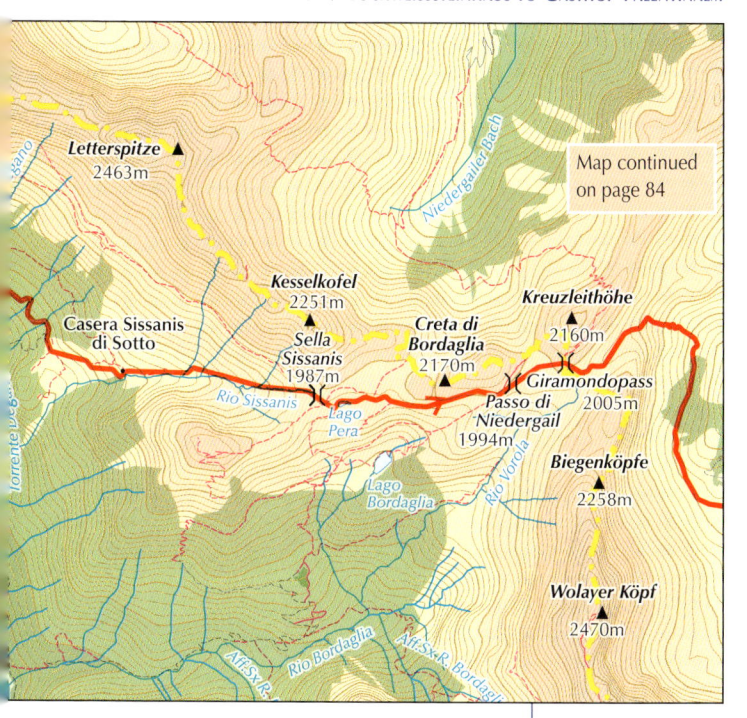

junction, leave the trees and arrive at a semi-abandoned farmstead, the **Casera Sissanis di Sotto** (1684m).

Mountain dairy farm Casera Fleons di Sotto

The Karnischer Höhenweg

The **Casera Sissanis di Sotto** is the gateway to a beautiful and tranquil valley, the Val di Sissanis. Expect to see huge flocks of sheep enjoying the bounty on the hillside. One of the buildings has been restored and is often occupied by shepherds.

From the farmstead, continue east along a well-defined path through potentially tall grass up to the **Sella Sissanis** pass (1987m). The climb is steady work and gains nearly 300m over a distance of 2.8km. ◂

> The views down the valley and back up to Öfner Joch and the mountains beyond are magnificent.

SELLA SISSANIS

The long climb up to Sella Sissanis

From the Sella Sissanis, the route enters a magical world. Immediately ahead is a tiny lake, the Lago Pera, behind which stands, like a sentinel, the Creta di Bordaglia (2170m). The lake is shallow, catches the sun, and is perhaps the best place on the Karnischer Höhenweg to take a dip.

The route is now once again close to the border and the World War I front line, and Italian information boards describe the fierce fighting that started in May 1915. In particular, they explain how the Italians, despite initiating the offensive, arrived too late to get the best positions, an experience that was repeated much to their cost along most of the front. The plinth on top of the little hill to the right is a memorial stone dedicated to Lieutenant Salvatore Pascoli, from the 10th Battalion Sharpshooter Cyclists, who was killed here in 1916.

The views to the south include Lago Bordaglia below, and beyond that a small range of mountains, the Terze–Siera, a dolomitic outlier from the main Carnic ridge. The highest mountain in Terze–Siera is Creta Forata (2462m).

Stage 4 – Austrian route: Hochweisssteinhaus to Gasthof Valentinalm

Lago Bordaglia with the South Carnic Alps beyond, seen from Sella Sissanis

After 600 metres, the path reaches a junction with the 142. Ignore the turn-offs and continue on a slightly exposed path across a bank of scree for 500 metres to a low ridge, the **Passo di Niedergail** (1994m), and some old Austrian trenchworks. After following an almost flat path through a lovely green valley, the route arrives at the **Giramondopass** (2005m), where it once again crosses the border and re-enters Austria.

From the pass, head north-east down a gully and then turn east on a steep zigzagging descent of the open grassy side of a valley. After descending for 300m, follow the path as it swings south into trees and contours around the head of the valley. Leaving the trees, swing north-west, crossing a boulder field and a meadow which in the summer will be full of grazing brown-and-white cattle. At a **junction with a dirt road** (1680m), turn right onto the dirt road and start a steady ascent south-east. ▶

Stay on the dirt road as it ascends and then, annoyingly, descends. After 1.5km, the 403 **leaves the dirt road** (1813m), makes a direct 120m ascent of the hillside and then rejoins the dirt road. This pre-lunch sting in the tale may be too much, so, if you're tired, stick to the slower,

The views across the valley are excellent. To the south-east are the northern flanks of Monte Coglians (2789m).

81

THE KARNISCHER HÖHENWEG

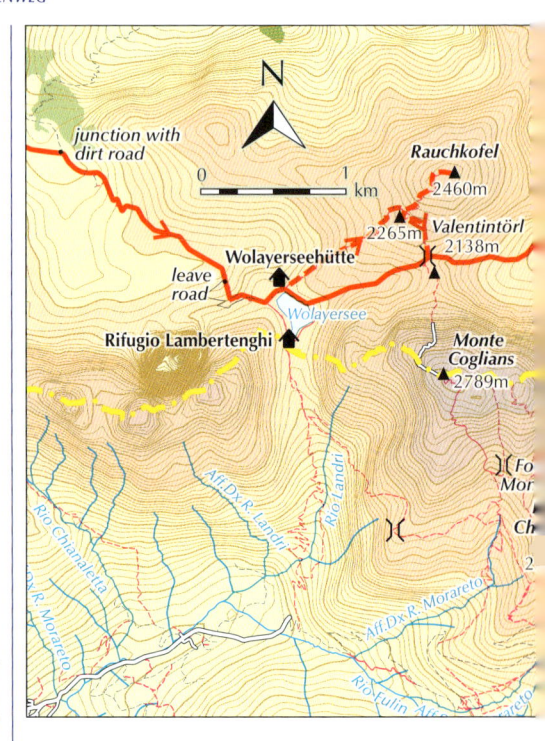

The beautifully located Wolayerseehütte, with war memorial behind

STAGE 4 – AUSTRIAN ROUTE: HOCHWEISSSTEINHAUS TO GASTHOF VALENTINALM

less direct dirt road, which continues on a more leisurely switchback route up the hillside to where the direct route comes in from the left. Follow the dirt road east to the **Wolayerseehütte** (1959m).

> The **Wolayerseehütte** (tel +43 (0)720 346141 www.wolayerseehuette-lesachtal.at) is another beautifully located hut and one that has recently benefited from comprehensive modernisation. As well as 40 dormitory beds, it has 24 beds in rooms of varying sizes, including rooms with just two beds. The hut is popular with Germans and Austrians, many of whom regard it as the best on the Karnischer Höhenweg. If you're not staying

The Karnischer Höhenweg

> **EDUARD PICHL**
>
> The Wolayerseehütte used to be named the Eduard Pichl Hut. Eduard Pichl was a key figure in the development of the German Alpine Club (which until after World War II was a single organisation covering the German-speaking world, with the largest membership of any recreational club in the world). A German nationalist and pre-war politician in Vienna, Pichl fought in World War I and after three years in captivity served as a mountain instructor. After the war, he worked on cataloguing the wartime supply routes in the mountains and is credited with spotting their tourist potential.
>
> Pichl was also anti-Semitic and a proto-Nazi, and was a close friend and biographer of Georg Schönerer, whose work influenced Adolf Hitler. In 1921, he became chair of the Austrian Section of the German Alpine Club and was responsible for the inclusion of an Aryan clause, effectively outlawing Jewish membership. (Individual clubs, including Vienna, had adopted such clauses before the War.) The Jewish membership (a third of the total membership), re-formed as the Danubia Section, but through the 1920s Jews were progressively excluded from club resources.
>
> The Alpine Club became completely enmeshed in the Nazi state, was proscribed by the Allies in 1945 and was only allowed to re-form as separate German and Austrian clubs in 1952. Post-war attempts were made to revive the Danubia Section but their ranks had been completely decimated by the Holocaust. The Austrian Alpine Club faced up to its history with difficulty, and it was not until 2002 that the hut named after Eduard Pichl in 1923 changed its name to the Wolayerseehütte.

At this point, you need to decide whether to walk the Austrian or the Italian route. The Italian route is described in Stages 4A and 5A–C.

the night, its modern and very efficient restaurant makes it a good place to grab some food before heading on to either the Gasthof Valentinalm or the Rifugio Marinelli.

If you prefer an Italian hut, the **Rifugio Lambertenghi Romanin** (tel +39 0433 786074 www.rifugiolambertenghi.it) is just a few hundred metres away across the border. Named after an Italian lieutenant who died here in 1915, it is even bigger than the Wolayerseehütte and has 94 beds, again in a variety of rooms. Another modern hut, it offers Italian rather than Austrian cuisine. The hut is owned by the Italian Alpine Association, and discounts for all Alpine Club members apply.

Optional ascent of Rauchkofel – moderate

If you spend the night at either the Wolayerseehütte or the Rifugio Lambertenghi and intend to stay on the Austrian side of the border, there is time next day to climb Rauchkofel (2460m) on the way to the Gasthof Valentinalm. It will add 1hr 30min to what is otherwise a 3hr walk and involves an extra 200m of climbing. It is not difficult, although it does include a cable-assisted stretch on the final approach to the summit.

From the Wolayerseehütte, take path 438 to **Rauchkofel** summit. Retrace your steps from the summit but instead of returning to the Wolayerseehütte turn left onto the 437. This takes you to the pass at **Valentintörl**, where you rejoin the 403.

Main route

From the Wolayerseehütte (if you are not climbing Rauchkofel), head round the lake to its eastern side. Follow the 403 and geotrail on a path climbing up the grassy side of a gully to the pass at **Valentintörl** (2138m). It's a 200m climb to what is the highest point on this stage and will take about 45min. ▶

> On both sides of the pass, expect to encounter snow.

The **Wolayersee** and surrounding area are particularly interesting in terms of both natural history and geology, forming the centrepiece of a nature reserve and featuring one of six geotrails in the Carnic Alps UNESCO Global Geopark. The lake itself dates back to the last ice age and was formed by a collapsed sinkhole. Two underground streams sustain the shallow lake, and a lining of mud prevents the water disappearing through layers of limestone, which in this part of the Alps are uniquely thick.

The **Valentintörl pass** between Rauchkofel and Monte Coglians sits at a point where three tectonic plates meet. The southern slopes of Rauchkofel, to the north-west of the pass, are built of younger, Carboniferous rocks (355–290 million years old); to the east, they border with shales from the Ordovician era (510–440 million years old). To the south, the high walls of Monte Coglians are composed of Devonian limestones (410–360 million years old).

On the descent from the pass, the path becomes easier to follow, eventually entering flower-filled meadows. After descending 450m over 2.4km, it joins a dirt road providing access to the Obere Valentinalm farmstead. As the road switchbacks its way down the valley, the path sometimes follows it and sometimes takes a more direct route, eventually bringing you to the **Gasthof Valentinalm** (1220m).

Gasthof Valentinalm

Stage 4 – Austrian route: Hochweisssteinhaus to Gasthof Valentinalm

MONTE COGLIANS AND KELLERSPITZEN

The line of mountains whose huge northern flanks dominate the southern side of the valley running up to the Valentintörl is the highest in the Carnic Alps. It was a source of 19th-century controversy whether the highest point was Monte Coglians or Kellerspitzen, with the Austrians claiming it was Kellerspitzen and the Italians claiming it was Monte Coglians. The Italians were proved right, with their mountain found to be 20m higher.

The two mountaintops were the location of bitter fighting in World War I. For once, the Italians, who had much easier routes up, got to the top first and occupied Monte Coglians. Meanwhile, the Austro-Hungarians tried to occupy the summit of Kellerspitzen and, despite the obvious difficulties of the approach, somehow succeeded in doing so. In the notorious winter of 1916, the whole north face of Kellerspitzen became a sheet of ice and the commander, against the orders of his generals, abandoned it. His fate is unknown.

The **Gasthof Valentinalm** (tel +43 (0)4715 92215 www.valentinalm.at) is a privately owned mountain inn providing a range of different types of accommodation, all excellent value. For the price-conscious, this includes accommodation in a dormitory. It's a comfortable, friendly place, providing food in the classic Austrian style.

STAGE 4A
Italian route: Hochweißsteinhaus to Rifugio Marinelli

Start	Hochweißsteinhaus
Distance	19.9km
Ascent/Descent	1360m/1100m
Difficulty	Challenging
Walking time	8hr 50min
Maximum altitude	2230m
Refreshments	Wolayerseehütte reached after 6hr
Routefinding	Good waymarking throughout

After crossing the exposed scree below the Rifugio Lambertenghi Romanin, Stage 4A embarks upon a sustained stretch of cable- and ladder-assisted walking known as the Sentiero Spinotti. Nervous walkers or those without a head for heights should avoid this stage, but if neither of these qualifications apply, the walk is a delight. It is a popular excursion for Italians so if it's a sunny Saturday in August, expect to share the experience with others. If you have walked from the Hochweißsteinhaus and had lunch at the Wolayerseehütte, it will probably be mid to late afternoon before you start, the light could be perfect and the views breathtaking.

The climb comes in two parts. The first part is the toughest and most exposed and involves almost constant use of cables (which are well maintained and in excellent condition). Next comes a long and easy walk around a huge bank of scree before a final cable-assisted climb to a grassy saddle. Although all the hard work is now done, there is still another hour's walking before arriving at the wonderful Rifugio Marinelli.

ALTERNATIVE SCHEDULES

The first part of this stage, from the Hochweißsteinhaus to the Wolayerseehütte, is described in Stage 4. The route directions below start from the Wolayerseehütte.

STAGE 4A – ITALIAN ROUTE: HOCHWEISSSTEINHAUS TO RIFUGIO MARINELLI

Paths to the top of Monte Coglians (2789m), the highest mountain in the Carnic Alps, lead off from this stage. It is, however, a tough 4hr round trip so you'll need to stay an extra night at the Wolayerseehütte or Rifugio Marinelli in order to attempt it (or it could be included as one of the alternative schedules described in Stage 5A).

From the Wolayerseehütte, head south along the western side of the lake, over the little ridge to **Rifugio Lambertenghi Romanin** (1955m). Continue along the dirt road, passing underneath the hut's supply cableway, to a junction with a signpost marked as route 145, Sentiero R. Spinotti. Take this path and follow it down across a field of scree formed from the huge cliffs of Monte Coglians looming above.

On the other side of the scree, the climb looks a little intimidating and it isn't immediately apparent how the cliffs will be climbed. Continue on the path, which is well defined, to a crack in the rocks, a chimney, and the escape route. With the help of **sustained cables** and a ladder, the first obstacle is quickly overcome and provides morale-boosting preparation for the challenges ahead. Gaining nearly 200m crossing the west-facing flank of Monte Coglians, the path levels out, swings

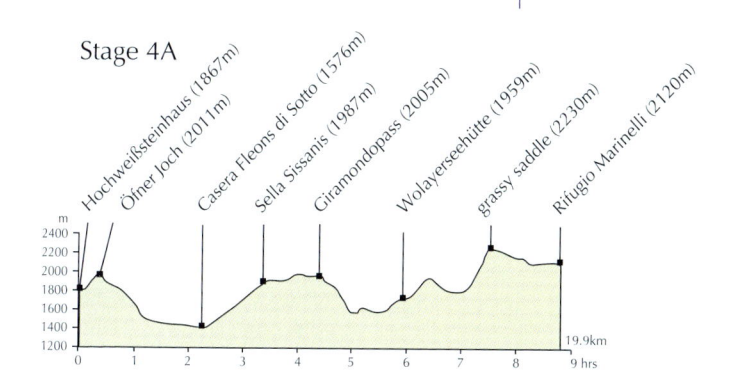

Stage 4A

THE KARNISCHER HÖHENWEG

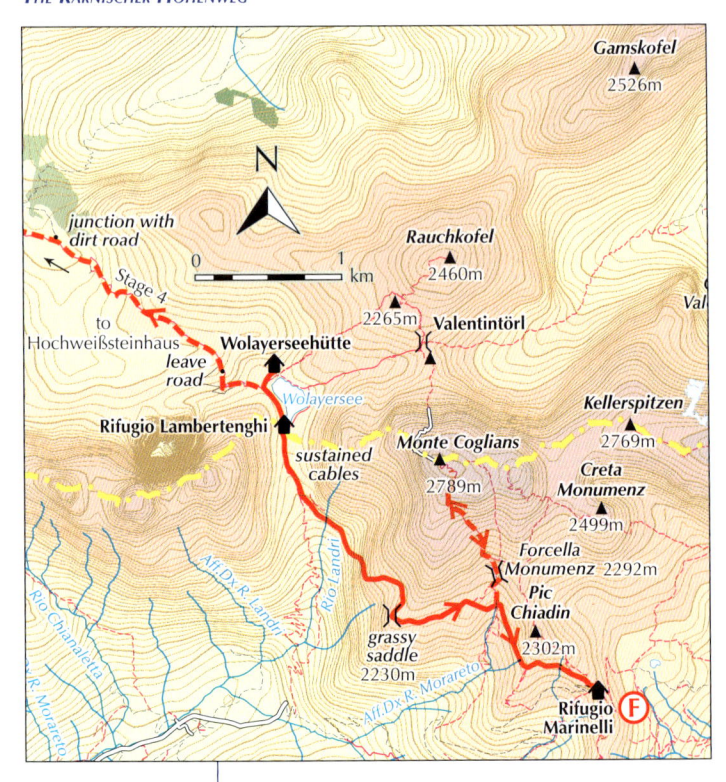

> Although the rest of the stage is not as exacting, there is still an hour's walking to complete before arriving at Rifugio Marinelli.

north and arcs around a high-level path crossing a huge south-facing scree slope. On the other side, after a little more cable-assisted climbing, it arrives at a **grassy saddle** (2230m) – a great place to stop, take pictures and pat yourself on the back. Looking back at the scree path, you'll be amazed at what you've just done. ◄

Continue east along a well-defined path, rocky at times, through a grassy limestone landscape on the south-facing slopes of Monte Coglians. After about 800 metres, the path descends gently and, after a short stretch of cable-assisted walking, crosses one then another path heading up to Monte Coglians. Climbing onto a ridge

STAGE 4A – ITALIAN ROUTE: HOCHWEISSSTEINHAUS TO RIFUGIO MARINELLI

formed of dark volcanic rock, alien in an otherwise limestone terrain, follow the path south-east to the **Rifugio Marinelli** (2120m).

> My alpine hiking experience suggests that Italian huts are more likely than the huts in Austria to put out the welcome mat. Less concerned with rules and regulations than their cousins across the border, they seem friendlier. The **Rifugio Marinelli** (tel +39 0433 779177 www.rifugiomarinelli.com) is a really good example and despite much competition is my favourite hut in all of the Alps. Although the huts visited so far have done the job, Rifugio Marinelli, despite comparable facilities, feels cosy and like a home from home. The food is rustic,

On the Sentiero Spinotti

hearty Italian, really outstanding and a big improvement on Austrian hut cuisine.

George and Maria run the hut in a light, friendly way (George looks after the wine and Maria everything else), and Maria, who speaks excellent English, is a mine of information and will help make forward bookings if you can't speak Italian. Although the hut can be busy at weekends (if it is, get quickly into the shower – the hot water doesn't last long), it's otherwise usually quiet. The Rifugio Marinelli has 50 beds, including some in small rooms.

It addition to its friendly atmosphere and exceptional food, **Rifugio Marinelli** provides one of the best viewpoints on the Karnischer Höhenweg. Enjoying a drink outside and looking east, you can see the next four days of walking laid out on a plate. To the left, framed inside the immediate ridge of mountains, and a white pyramid in the evening sun, is Polinik (2332m). To the right of that and closer, just beyond the Plöckenpass, are the flat tops of Kleiner Pal (1867m) and Großer Pal (1814m), and behind them the sharper and taller summit of the Creta di Timau (2217m). Further to the right, and much more distant, is the last big limestone peak on the Carnic ridge, and one of its most beautiful, Trogkofel (2279m). Last but not least, to the southeast, resembling the Dolomites, are the Julian Alps.

Optional ascent of Monte Coglians – challenging
Many people will find the scree fields and rock scrambling near the top of Monte Coglians (2789m) challenging, but the reward – views from the top of the highest mountain in the Carnic Alps – is immense.

From Rifugio Marinelli, return along the grassy slopes of the volcanic ridge (heading back the way you came) to the first junction with a path up to Monte Coglians. Leave the main route, turn right and head north to a low pass, the **Forcella Monumenz** (2292m). Traverse the south-facing

Stage 4A – Italian route: Hochweisssteinhaus to Rifugio Marinelli

A tough climb up to Monte Coglians

slope and start to ascend the scree, eventually reaching a small notch between the main summit and the east summit. Turn left and climb a rocky slope to the main summit of **Monte Coglians**. Retrace your steps to **Rifugio Marinelli**.

> The cloud was swirling around the summit of **Monte Coglians** on my last visit, and while I missed out on the views (some claim you can see the Mediterranean), I did at least have the place to myself. It's a spooky place with well-preserved dugouts and other wartime remains. With vertical cliffs descending from the mountain's northern side, it's almost inconceivable that there was any fighting here, but there was. After looking in the trenches and dugouts, imagining life up here 100 years ago, it's impossible to do anything other than ring the Peace Bell.

The Karnischer Höhenweg

STAGE 5
Austrian route: Gasthof Valentinalm to Zollnerseehütte

Start	Gasthof Valentinalm
Distance	19km
Ascent/Descent	1440m/950m
Difficulty	Moderate
Walking time	7hr 30min
Maximum altitude	2150m
Refreshments	None, picnic essential
Routefinding	Generally good waymarking: follow the 403

On this stage, the character of the walk starts to change. The stage can be broken down into three parts, each with its own distinct characteristics. The first part, up to the Obere Spielbodenalm, is a walk through larch and pine, pleasant enough but lacking the drama experienced on the first four days. After a steep climb, the second part travels around a huge wide valley whose lovely grassy hillsides are wonderful in the sunshine but bleak, desolate and almost certainly empty if it's raining. If there is a bit of mist or cloud about, obscuring the huge mountains in the distance, it feels like a walk through high moors in the north of England. Finally, having crossed the pass at Ködertörl (and the border and front line), the walk drops into a much tighter valley following the remains of a decaying but still beautifully engineered military road, before making the final climb up to the Zollnerseehütte.

ALTERNATIVE SCHEDULES

For a more dramatic walk to the Zollnerseehütte, consider heading south from the Plöckenhaus (on the Austrian side) towards the Plöckenpass (on the border). On the way, the path hits the route up to the World War I Open-air Museum described in 5B below. Stage 5 is part of the original Karnischer Höhenweg and still walked by most Germans and Austrians, but the attractions of the alternative route described in 5A–C are obvious.

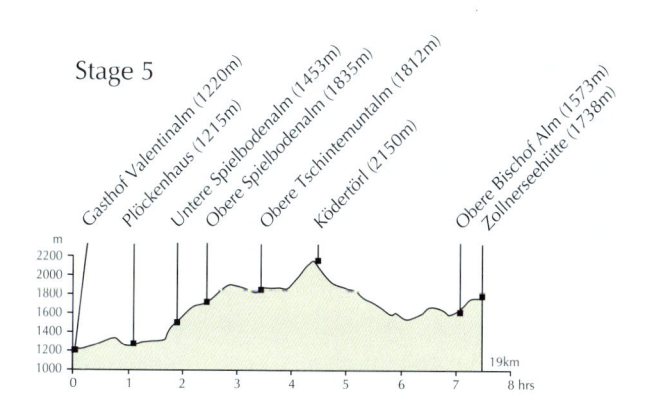

Stage 5 – Austrian route: Gasthof Valentinalm to Zollnerseehütte

Stage 5

Gasthof Valentinalm (1220m)
Plöckenhaus (1215m)
Untere Spielbodenalm (1453m)
Obere Spielbodenalm (1835m)
Obere Tschintemuntalm (1812m)
Ködertörl (2150m)
Obere Bischof Alm (1573m)
Zollnerseehütte (1738m)

19km / 8 hrs

From the Gasthof Valentinalm, head down south-west to a bridge, cross it, and climb gently east along a path through beech trees for 1.5km to a junction. Ignore the path south and continue east with the 403, now descending, to emerge near a lake 500 metres later. Continue east to the **Plöckenhaus** (1215m). ▶

To connect with the World War I Open-air Museum – moderate

To connect with the route described in Stage 5B and walk to the Zollnerseehütte via the World War I Open-air Museum, cross the road and head south past the little wooden chapel. Picking up the 434-1, head up through trees for about 500 metres to what looks like a boat without its superstructure but is, in fact, a restored World War I **machine gun post**. Turn left and climb along the route described in Stage 5B.

Join a dirt road opposite the Plöckenhaus and continue east. The building to the south of the route houses World War I winding gear for the **cable car** that was used to supply troops positioned around Kleiner Pal. Continue east to a junction with the 436, reached after 400 metres, and bear left following the southern shore of a small **lake** (the

The Plöckenhaus used to be a hotel but now only serves food and even then is unlikely to be open first thing in the morning.

THE KARNISCHER HÖHENWEG

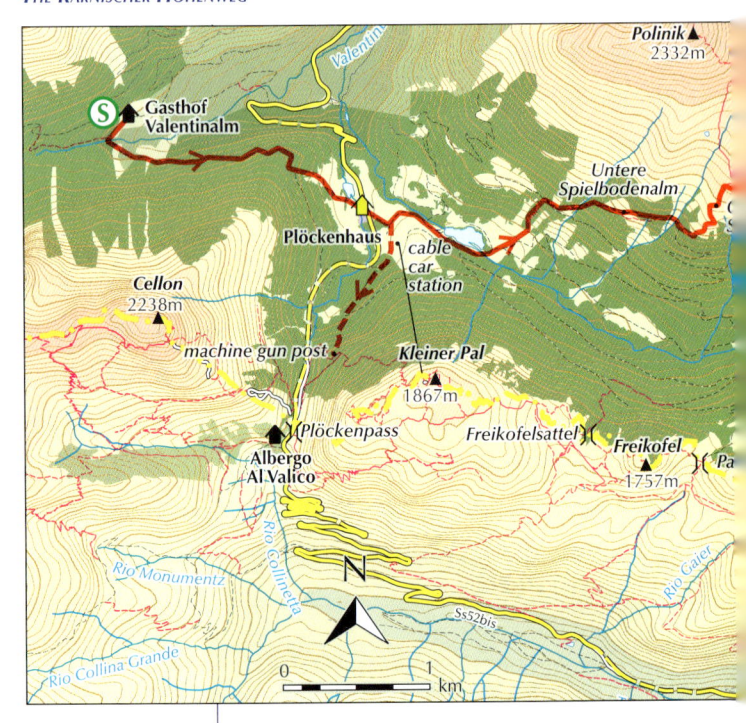

Grünsee). After another 400 metres, leave the dirt road (there is a sign) and, passing through a gate, follow an indistinct path north-east as it climbs across a meadow. Stones in the field are marked but it's easy to get confused with poles for a winter cross-country ski run. Leave the meadow after 200 metres, re-enter the trees and follow a path zigzagging its way north up the side of the valley.

After a steep ascent (climbing 150m), turn right onto a forest road and then, after 20 metres, left onto a path crossing a meadow before heading back into trees. Follow the path for 400 metres and after crossing a gully emerge into an alpine meadow with a shepherds' hut in the corner (**Untere Spielbodenalm**, 1453m). Continue past the hut along a forest road for 400 metres and, as

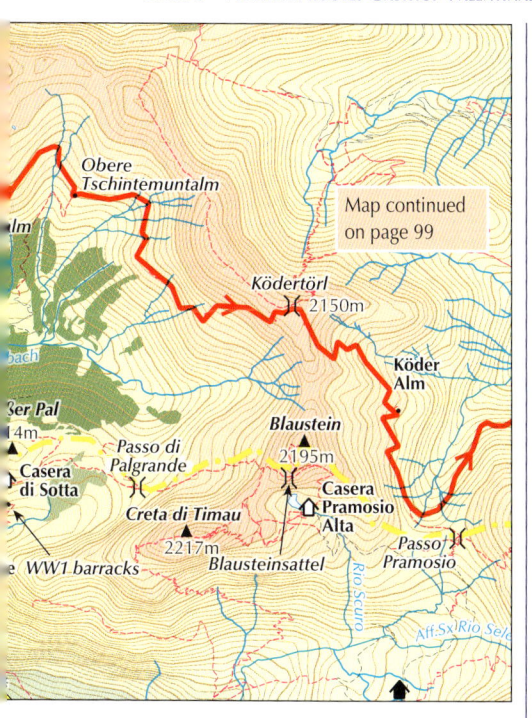

STAGE 5 – AUSTRIAN ROUTE: GASTHOF VALENTINALM TO ZOLLNERSEEHÜTTE

it swings south and down, leave it and turn left onto a path. After 200 metres the path swings north and emerges into open meadow/moor. Continue to climb on a switchback path across the hillside to the **Obere Spielbodenalm** (1835m) for a well-deserved break and some fresh mountain water. ▸

Leaving the Obere Spielbodenalm, continue up the hillside for another 100 metres to a junction with route 430 up to Polinik (2332m). Ignore the junction and turn right, following a lovely path that contours its way east, high along the side of the valley. After 1.4km and a gentle descent, cross a stream. Head south-east for 800 metres, climbing gently through gorse, dwarf pine and alder thicket to the ruins of a farmstead, the **Obere**

As the walk leaves the trees, its character improves. Entering huge south-facing upland alpine meadows, there are, once again, massive views to enjoy.

Obere Spielbodenalm – Cellon in the background

The trenches at Ködertörl and the strands of barbed wire that decorate the sign show that the path has returned to the World War I front line.

The route from Kleiner Pal and the World War I Open-air Museum also joins Stage 5 here and the two routes journey together to the Zollnerseehütte.

Tschintemuntalm (1812m). Still following a contouring path, swing east and then south around the head of the main valley before starting a sustained climb to the pass, the **Ködertörl** (2150m), the highest point on this stage. From the Obere Tschintemuntalm to the pass takes about 90min. ◄

From the pass, head south-east. The descent, gentle at first, gets steeper as the path switchbacks its way down the mountainside. The other side of the valley should now be visible, along with the old military road etched perfectly into the side of the mountain. Some 1.5km after crossing Ködertörl, the path approaches an old shepherds' hut, the **Köder Alm** (1831m), before again switchbacking its way deep into the western side of the valley and over a stream. About 1km after passing the Köder Alm, the path reaches a junction with a path coming down from the east from Passo Pramosio. ◄

STAGE 5 – AUSTRIAN ROUTE: GASTHOF VALENTINALM TO ZOLLNERSEEHÜTTE

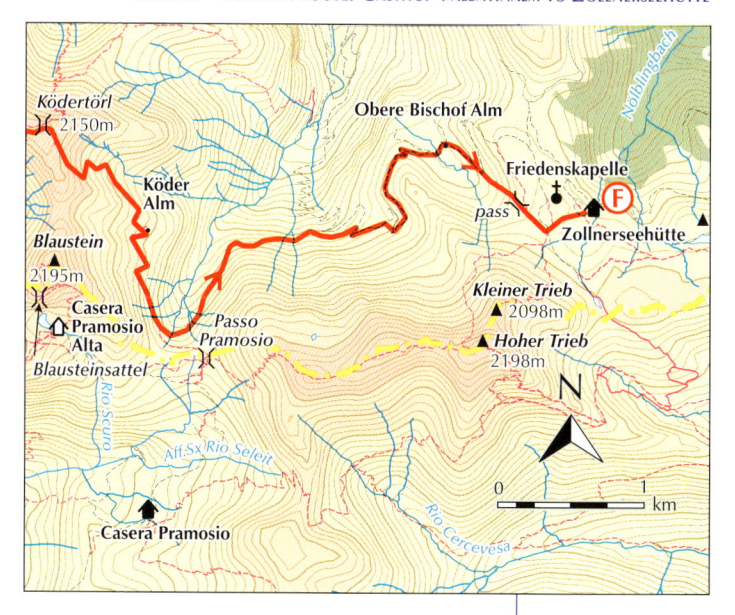

From the junction, the route turns north and follows a beautifully engineered military road that descends gently along the side of the valley. Most of it still survives, 100 years after its construction, but some short stretches have been lost to landslides and care needs to be taken when bridging the gaps. After 2km and after swinging east, the old military road reaches a junction with route 426. ▶

The road now starts to climb. After 250 metres, a turn onto an indistinct path cuts off a long switchback. If you miss the turn, stay on the dirt road and follow it as it swings north into trees and then east down to a stream and a farmstead, the **Obere Bischof Alm** (1573m). Ignore the turn-off to the 424 and continue south-east past the farmstead along a path through meadows (past a sign to the Rossa Alm) and up to a **pass** at the end of the little valley. Although short, the climb to the pass is surprisingly steep.

> Route 426 leads north into the Gailtal (Gail Valley) and a frequent train service.

99

The memorial chapel at Zollnerseehütte

After crossing the pass, head north-east across meadows (often waterlogged) for 250 metres to the **Zollnerseehütte** (1738m).

The **Zollnerseehütte** (mob +43 (0)676 9602209 www.alpenverein.at/zollnerseehuette) is a small, intimate and very pleasant mountain hut. Facing south-south-west, the tables either side of the main door make a perfect location for a late afternoon beer, well deserved after a long day's walk. There is a dormitory with 28 beds, and two smaller rooms, each with four beds.

The **Friedenskapelle**, the Peace Chapel, located next door to the Zollnerseehütte, was built in the 1980s in commemoration of fallen soldiers of World War I, some of whom are interred here.

STAGE 5A
Italian route: Rifugio Marinelli to Plöckenpass

Start	Rifugio Marinelli
Distance	6.3km
Ascent/Descent	100m/760m
Difficulty	Moderate
Walking time	2hr 15min
Maximum altitude	2120m
Refreshments	None
Routefinding	Easy

Stages 5A, B and C complete the Italian variant to the Karnischer Höhenweg. Stage 5A is relatively short and, apart from an interesting climb over a saddle from one valley to another, is downhill all the way. It's an easy and pleasant walk through rocky alpine flower meadows, with the huge cliffs of Monte Coglians providing a dramatic backdrop. This short stage makes it possible to spend time in the World War I Open-air Museum in Stage 5B.

ALTERNATIVE SCHEDULE

A short day provides the opportunity to consider one or the other of two variants. The first involves heading back along the trail (the way you came) and climbing Monte Coglians (see route description at end of Stage 4A). If the weather is reasonable, climbing the biggest mountain in the Carnic Alps is highly recommended. If an additional 4hr is too much, consider adding the ascent of Cellon to the schedule (see below). This 620m climb adds 3hr 15min to the day.

From Rifugio Marinelli, follow a well-defined path (the 146) south-east along the eastern side of a ridge. After nearly 300 metres, turn sharply north and descend into the valley, swinging east after another 300 metres. Continue east to a signpost and, still on the 146, turn

THE KARNISCHER HÖHENWEG

The wonderful Rifugio Marinelli with Monte Coglians behind

north-east onto a path and continue across the valley. Follow this path for 300 metres across a rocky high-level meadow; ignore a sign on a rock for the 171 and continue east on the 146. Below and to the south-east of the path is a lake. Continue for another 1.4km along the path as it descends gently through gullies and more open boulder-strewn meadows with occasional alpenrose (ignoring a path to the right on the way).

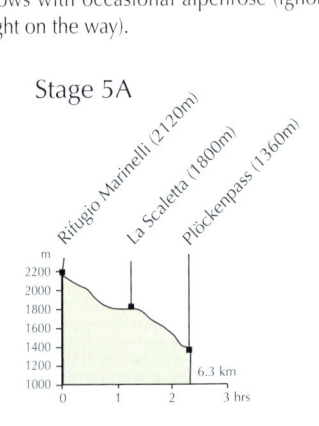

Stage 5A

Rifugio Marinelli (2120m)
La Scaletta (1800m)
Plöckenpass (1360m)

6.3 km

STAGE 5A – ITALIAN ROUTE: RIFUGIO MARINELLI TO PLÖCKENPASS

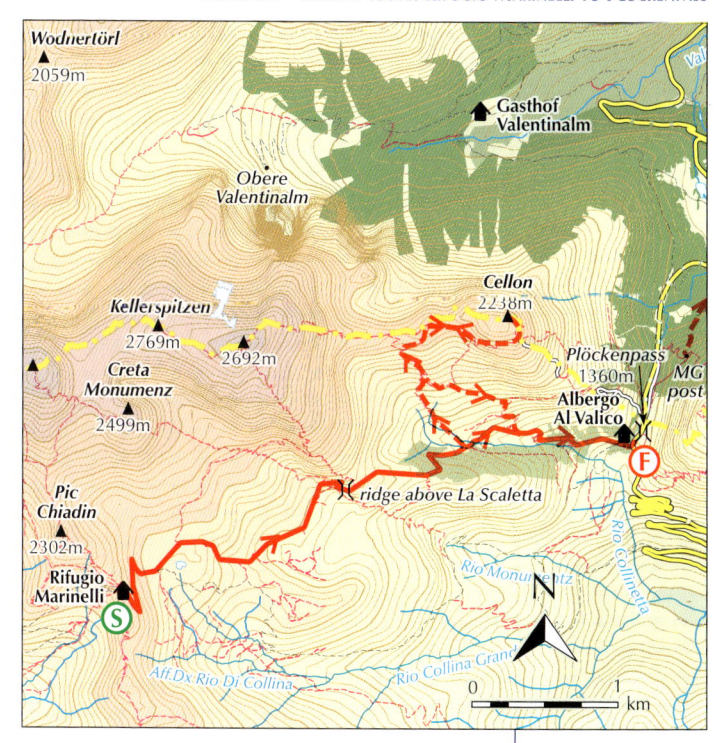

As the path approaches the cliffs climbing up to Monte Coglians, it reaches a junction with the 149 and continues east. After another 100 metres or so along a narrow path, the route swings into a cavern (**La Scaletta**, 1800m), and climbs up along steps with help from a cable through what is almost a tunnel, out onto a **ridge**. Climb along the ridge for about 100 metres before starting to descend. You have now crossed a saddle into the next valley. After 700 metres, there is a junction with a path climbing south; ignore it and continue on the 146. Switchbacking towards the north down into a wide valley, the path reaches a river, the Rio Collinetta (1690m), and a junction with the 147 after 500 metres. ▶ The path

> The junction with the 147 marks the start of the climb up to Cellon: see below.

The route enters a cavern, La Scaletta, where it climbs up steps to a ridge

continues east along an increasingly wooded path down to the **Plöckenpass** (1360m) and the **Albergo Al Valico**.

With open borders, the significance of the **Plöckenpass** has declined, but historically it has always been a strategic point for invaders heading north or south: Napoleon came through here on his way into Carinthia in 1809. In 1915–17, in order for either side to have broken through this part of the front line in significant numbers, they would have had to cross this pass, so each side fortified it heavily to prevent the other side from doing so. Cellon on the western side and Kleiner Pal on its eastern side were the scenes of an intense stalemate.

The eastern flanks of **Cellon** have some spectacular via ferratas and other features, including the Cellon Stollen, a 180-metre-long tunnel with a 120m internal climb. Cellon is also famous for its avalanche gully where, over a span of 60 metres of rock, fossils visible in the rock provide a geological timeline of the transition from the Ordovician era to the Silurian period (a period of 60 million years). This unique site can be visited by a geotrail, where a

STAGE 5A – ITALIAN ROUTE: RIFUGIO MARINELLI TO PLÖCKENPASS

series of information boards document the geological history of the world. The trail starts opposite the car park at the Plöckenpass and takes at least 30min.

The **Albergo Al Valico** (tel +39 0433 779326) keeps a low profile but despite a limited web presence manages to thrive. Its main business is its excellent restaurant but it has accommodation too. Booking can be a challenge unless you speak Italian: on my first visit they were full, although this may have been a communication failure; I managed to get a booking on my most recent trip, but only through Rifugio Marinelli. There is no email but they do answer the phone, so you could ask the staff at Rifugio Marinelli to make the booking for you.

If you do have booking problems, then the **Gasthof Valentinalm** (tel +43 (0)4715 92215 www.valentinalm.at), on the Austrian side of the border, is the obvious alternative. It is a privately owned mountain inn providing a range of different types of accommodation (including dormitory), all excellent value. It's a comfortable, friendly place, providing food in the classic Austrian style. To get there from the Albergo Al Valico, take the route north towards the Austrian entrance to the World War I Open-air Museum, but instead of heading up to Kleiner Pal, continue to the Plöckenhaus and then follow the 403 west to the Gasthof Valentinalm. It's an easy 4.5km walk.

Optional ascent of Cellon – moderate to challenging

The junction with the 147, signposted 'Cresta Verde 1hr 30min', marks the start of a climb up to Cellon (2238m), the last summit on the Coglians ridge. The 147 heads north-west and then turns east before reaching the Cresta Verde and continuing to **Cellon** summit. On the return trip, head back to the junction with the Cresta Verde route, continue down the 147 but then turn left to take a slightly more direct route to the **Plöckenpass**. The ascent of Cellon adds 3hr 15min to the stage.

STAGE 5B
Italian route: Plöckenpass to Casera Pramosio

Start	Plöckenpass
Distance	11.2km
Ascent/Descent	1300m/1030m
Difficulty	Challenging
Walking time	7hr 15min
Maximum altitude	2101m
Refreshments	None
Routefinding	Signage through the World War I Open-air Museum can be confusing

Stage 5B visits the most contested part of the World War I front line in the Carnic Alps, where fighting was close and personal, and includes a walk through the World War I Open-air Museum. This is not a 'museum' in the conventional sense, where exhibits are curated and explained. There is no entrance fee and very little in the way of facilities, but a lot to stimulate the imagination. Getting to the top involves a 300m climb so don't expect a queue to get in.

The museum centres on the Austro-Hungarian positions around Kleiner Pal, but the Italian positions on Freikofel are also complex and well preserved. The Austro-Hungarian positions have been maintained by the Dolomitenfreunde (Friends of the Dolomites) in conjunction with an excellent museum in the village of Kötschach, in the valley to the north. The Italian positions are looked after by an equivalent Italian organisation, the Associazione Amici Alpi Carniche (Association of Friends of the Carnic Alps), who are also working on a restoration of barracks and trenches around the Passo Cavallo.

World War I dominates the stage but there are other things to see. After the Passo Cavallo, the route passes through a lovely and surprisingly remote alpine valley before making a long and tough climb up to a pass, the Blausteinsattel.

Although described as part of the Italian route, 5B stays close to the front line, straddling the border before finishing in Italy. The challenging part of the stage is the descent from Freikofel to the Passo Cavallo: it is steep, dense with earthworks and has some short cabled stretches.

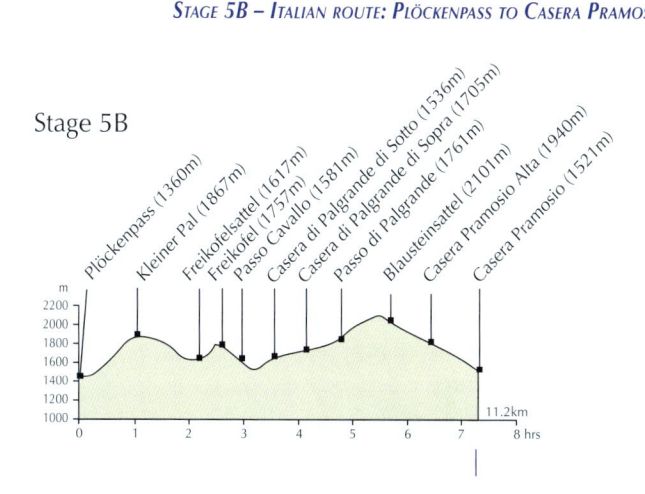

Stage 5B – Italian route: Plöckenpass to Casera Pramosio

Stage 5B

Plöckenpass (1360m), Kleiner Pal (1867m), Freikofelsattel (1617m), Freikofel (1757m), Passo Cavallo (1581m), Casera di Palgrande di Sotto (1536m), Casera di Palgrande di Sopra (1705m), Passo di Palgrande (1761m), Blausteinsattel (2101m), Casera Pramosio Alta (1940m), Casera Pramosio (1521m)

11.2km
8 hrs

ALTERNATIVE SCHEDULES

Casera Pramosio is a lovely place to stay but involves a walk south down the valley along a concrete road. If this descent is avoided, it is possible to get from the Plöckenpass to the Zollnerseehütte in 9hr 45min. Not many would attempt this, but by missing the climb over Freikofel and the trenchworks at Passo Cavallo, thus saving 90min, it might become more tempting. If you choose to do this, turn left off the concrete road about 1km after Casera Pramosio Alta and take the path heading up to Passo Pramosio to join the Austrian route, from where it is about 2hr to the Zollnerseehütte.

FIGHTING AT THE PLÖCKENPASS

The trenches, shelters, and caverns restored by the Dolomitenfreunde represent the status of the front line in October 1917, when the Italian army had to give up the whole Eastern front in the Alps after the Austro-Hungarian army broke through in the 12th Battle of Isonzo.

When Italy declared war on the Austro-Hungarian Empire in May 1915, the Italians occupied Kleiner Pal. After fierce fighting in the summer, the Austro-Hungarian army reconquered the mountain and drove the Italians back to Freikofel. Crucial parts of the Austrian lines, however, were exposed

The Karnischer Höhenweg

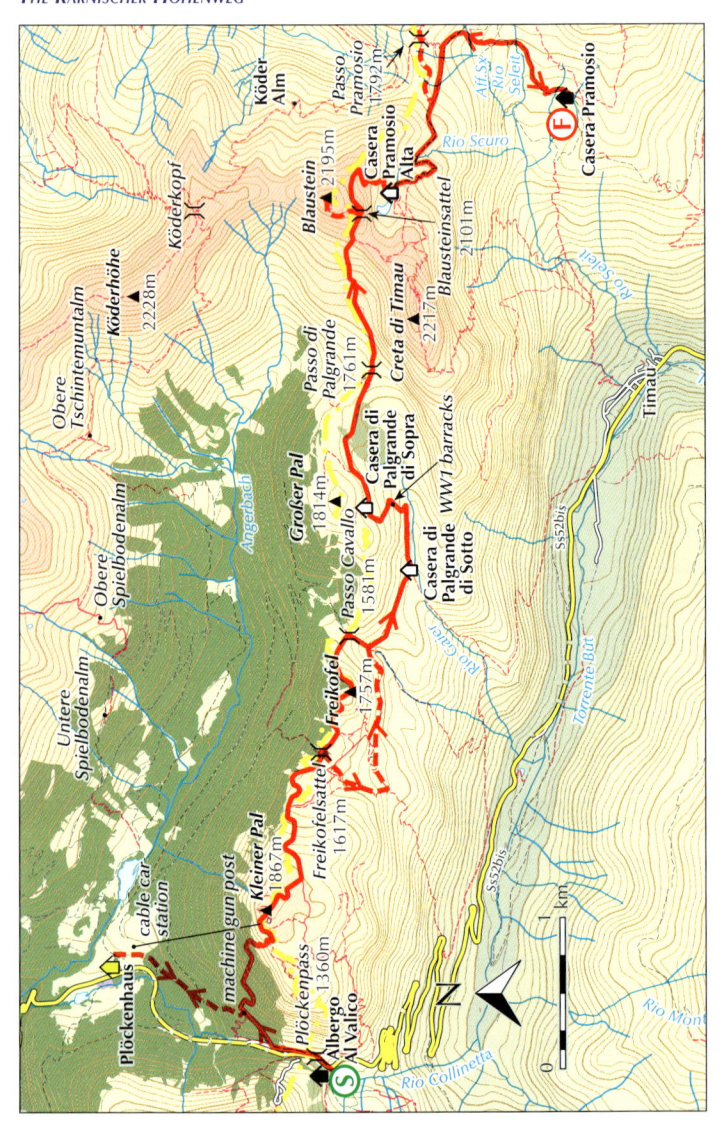

STAGE 5B – ITALIAN ROUTE: PLÖCKENPASS TO CASERA PRAMOSIO

Sleeping quarters on Kleiner Pal

to the Italian artillery, and the Italians caused serious losses and managed to reoccupy parts of Kleiner Pal.

Both sides then sought to gain the upper hand, with fighting continuing through to the following summer as each tried to dislodge the other from their positions on Kleiner Pal and Freikofel. The mutual loss of life was enormous but the gains were insignificant. The Austro-Hungarian position on Kleiner Pal was affected by what happened on the other side of the Plöckenpass, on Cellon. When the Italians captured Cellon, the Austro-Hungarian trenches were exposed to Italian artillery observers and the troops had to dig further into the rocks to gain shelter from the shelling. The same observers were also able to direct shelling down into the villages at Kötschach and Mauthen and the first civilians were killed in 1916 (the Italians were trying to hit two big Austro-Hungarian guns that had been disrupting their supply routes).

As both the Italian and the Austro-Hungarian general staffs focused their interest on the Isonzo line, the Carnic Alps turned into a defensive rather than offensive front line, and the numbers killed by fighting declined. In places, the front lines were no more than 30 metres apart and it's interesting to speculate on what form the coexistence took.

From the Albergo Al Valico, head north across the border into Austria along the main road. After 200 metres, join an access road on the right-hand side of a tunnel. After a few

THE KARNISCHER HÖHENWEG

Trenches with fire positions on Freikofel

This is where the link comes in from Gasthof Valentinalm, as described in Stage 5.

metres, turn right and follow yellow signs up through trees to a restored **machine gun post** (1480m) that looks like an upturned boat. ◄ Turn right at the machine gun post and continue east on the 434 on a zigzagging path up through trees. After a steep climb, the route reaches the front line.

There are **war relics** everywhere and the distractions make sticking to the path difficult. When you reach the front line, the main route continues east, but if you have plenty of time it is worth turning west to explore the trenchworks overlooking the Plöckenpass. When you've finished exploring, return to where the 434 joins the front line and pick up the main route east.

The lower station, complete with engine, is located near the Plöckenhaus.

Walk east for 100 metres to reach the restored upper station for the cable car. ◄ From the upper station, the

110

STAGE 5B – ITALIAN ROUTE: PLÖCKENPASS TO CASERA PRAMOSIO

route makes a gentle climb south-east to **Kleiner Pal** (1867m). There are numerous side routes from here, so if you are in a hurry you will need to use your GPS to follow the most direct route among the trenchworks. The direct route descends gently for about 1.6km to a pass, the **Freikofelsattel** (1617m).

The Freikofelsattel is an important junction, where you have the choice of ascending Freikofel (1757m) or bypassing it to the south. To ascend, follow the sign marked 436 to **Freikofel** summit. ▶ From the summit, continue east following a difficult path, exposed at times but with cables to help, down to a pass, the **Passo Cavallo** (1581m), where the route returns to Italy. Head south from the pass into a grassy valley. Immediately on the right is a path along an old military road; ignore it. Continue down the hill and turn right after 200 metres. To the right is a ruined building. ▶

The intensity of the trenchworks on **Freikofel** is a testament to its importance to the Italians. The proximity of the Austrian front line and the efforts taken to defend the position are obvious. Particularly interesting are the machine gun pits, enhanced with

The climb up its western side is not nearly as difficult as the climb down on the eastern side. To bypass Freikofel, follow the alternative below.

The alternative route bypassing Freikofel rejoins the main route here.

On Freikofel, looking towards Polinik

The Karnischer Höhenweg

concrete, the slits facing the enemy lines, and the tunnels hacked out of the rocks enabling soldiers to move from place to place in some safety. From the little summit, whose shallow northern face is still covered with hundreds of metres of rusty barbed wire, the Italians could check all the movements of the Habsburg troops below. The memorial on the summit dates back to the 1920s and was placed there by the Tolmezzo Battalion of the Alpini Corps.

On the descent to the **Passo Cavallo**, the mountainside is covered with ruins and barbed wire. At the pass itself, extensive restoration has been completed by Italian volunteers, including the reconstruction of barracks.

Alternative route bypassing Freikofel

To omit the ascent of Freikofel, follow the 436/402 south and down the hill. After about 200 metres, turn left onto the 401 and continue for about 400 metres east, rejoining the main route after its descent from the Passo Cavallo, just past some ruined buildings.

From where the two routes merge, continue east for 300 metres to an unmanned refuge, the **Casera di Palgrande di Sotto** (1536m), then head east along the side of a stream into an increasingly dramatic gorge. After 600 metres, turn north and climb up to the ruins of an Italian **World War I barracks**. Pass the barracks and follow a switchbacking path up to a larger unmanned refuge, the **Casera di Palgrande di Sopra** (1705m). Continue east from the refuge for 800 metres and over a pass, the **Passo di Palgrande** (1761m).

Head east along the northern flank of the main ridge. ◀ After 800 metres (and a climb of over 200m), you reach a junction with a path heading south up to the Creta di Timau (2217m). Ignore this junction and continue a steep climb to a ridge, the **Blausteinsattel** (2101m) – the highest point of the day. The ridge is just to the south of **Blaustein** (2195m), a summit worth climbing if the weather is fine. ◀

Below is the wide Angerbach Valley and to the north of the valley stands Polinik (2332m).

Follow the easy 200-metre path from the ridge to Blaustein summit. Retrace your steps to the ridge.

STAGE 5B – ITALIAN ROUTE: PLÖCKENPASS TO CASERA PRAMOSIO

From the ridge, and now back in Italy, head east and then south along a steeply descending but well-defined grassy path. To the west are the sheer white cliffs of the Blausteinsattel and below is a lovely lake, the Lago Avostanis, next to which is another unmanned refuge, the **Casera Pramosio Alta** (1940m). There are two huts called Casera Pramosio: one high (*alta*) and one low; the low one is manned.

From the Casera Pramosio Alta, follow a switchbacking road, initially dirt, then concrete, east. After 1km, the road reaches a junction with a path heading up to the Passo Pramosio (1792m). ▶ To continue to the very comfortable **Casera Pramosio** (1521m), just 30min away, ignore the junction and stay on the road. The descent follows the concrete road for most of its journey but helpfully takes a more direct route across switchbacks in a couple of places.

To reach the Zollnerseehütte in another 2hr 30min, turn left here to Passo Pramosio and follow Stage 5C directions from there to the Zollnerseehütte.

The **Casera Pramosio** (tel +39 0433 775757) is a lovely place. A working farm, producing cheese, it has an excellent restaurant and 20 beds. It's a popular lunchtime destination, particularly at weekends, but quiet in the evenings. The family who run it are very welcoming, but they speak no English and apparently their Italian is a distinct local dialect so booking can be a challenge. During the week they are unlikely to be full, but if you want to book ahead the staff at Rifugio Marinelli will help you.

A **memorial to Maria Plozner Mentil** is positioned on rocks next to the road on the approach to the Casera Pramosio. The metal engraving, based on a photograph, depicts women 'carriers' who, aged between 16 and 60, transported war materials on their backs up to the front line. Maria Plozner Mentil, who was killed by a sniper in February 1916, is depicted as a representative of all the civilians who lost their lives supporting the soldiers on the front line.

STAGE 5C
Italian route: Casera Pramosio to Zollnerseehütte

Start	Casera Pramosio
Distance	7km
Ascent/Descent	700m/500m
Difficulty	Moderate
Walking time	3hr
Maximum altitude	1792m
Refreshments	None
Routefinding	Easy

This is a short and relatively easy stage. After a steady climb up to the Passo Pramosio followed by a short descent, the Austrian and Italian routes come together for the journey to the Zollnerseehütte. This includes a lovely walk along the old military road and another short climb over a pass.

ALTERNATIVE SCHEDULES

The short day opens up the possibility of doing some extra climbing, and the ascent of Hoher Trieb is the obvious option. The ridge on the final approach to what is a stunning summit has some particularly interesting Italian World War I fortifications. The ascent is straightforward but getting down is more difficult. To avoid the challenging descent (two options), consider retracing your steps and following the main route over the Passo Pramosio.

Climbing Hoher Trieb and descending directly to the Zollnerseehütte adds 1hr 15min to Stage 5C. Although the south-facing 'sun terrace' at the Zollnerseehütte is an attractive place to while away an afternoon, the Straniger Alm (together with more cheesy delights) is only an easy 2hr walk away. Continuing to the Straniger Alm has the added benefit of reducing the time needed for Stage 6.

STAGE 5C – ITALIAN ROUTE: CASERA PRAMOSIO TO ZOLLNERSEEHÜTTE

Stage 5C

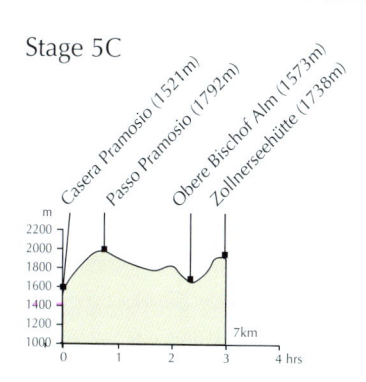

Retrace yesterday's descent for 1.3km, but leave the concrete road as it swings west around the head of the valley and take a path to the right. Continue along the path for 300 metres to the **Passo Pramosio** (1792m). From the pass, head west and descend to a junction with the 403 and the main Karnischer Höhenweg. ▸

Alternatively, to climb Hoher Trieb, head south-east from the pass: see Hoher Trieb variant below.

> On the approach to the pass, watch out for some **World War I tunnels** that go from one side of the ridge to the other. An original plaque on the side of one of the tunnel tells us who built it (the Second Alpini 222 Company), its length (68.5 metres) and its capacity in terms of men (380). If you're not afraid of ghosts (and the dark), you can walk through it and look out through a tiny portal into the valley on the other side.

From the junction with the 403, the route turns north and follows a beautifully engineered military road that descends gently along the side of the valley. Most of it still survives, 100 years after its construction, but some short stretches have been lost to landslides and care needs to be taken when bridging the gaps. After 2km and after swinging east, the old military road reaches a junction with route 426. ▸

Route 426 leads north into the Gailtal (Gail Valley) and a frequent train service.

115

THE KARNISCHER HÖHENWEG

The road now starts to climb. After 250 metres, a turn onto an indistinct path cuts off a long switchback. If you miss the turn, stay on the dirt road and follow it as it swings north into trees and then east down to a stream and a farmstead, the **Obere Bischof Alm** (1573m). Ignore the turn-off to the 424 and continue south-east past the farmstead along a path through meadows (past a sign to the Rossa Alm) and up to a **pass** at the end of the little valley. Although short, the climb to the pass is surprisingly steep.

After crossing the pass, head north-east across meadows (often waterlogged) for 250 metres to the **Zollnerseehütte** (1738m).

The **Zollnerseehütte** (mob +43 (0)676 9602209 www.alpenverein.at/zollnerseehuette) is a small, intimate and very pleasant mountain hut. Facing south-south-west, the tables either side of the main door make a perfect location for beer, strudel or both. There is a dormitory with 28 beds, and two smaller rooms, each with four beds.

Barracks on Hoher Trieb

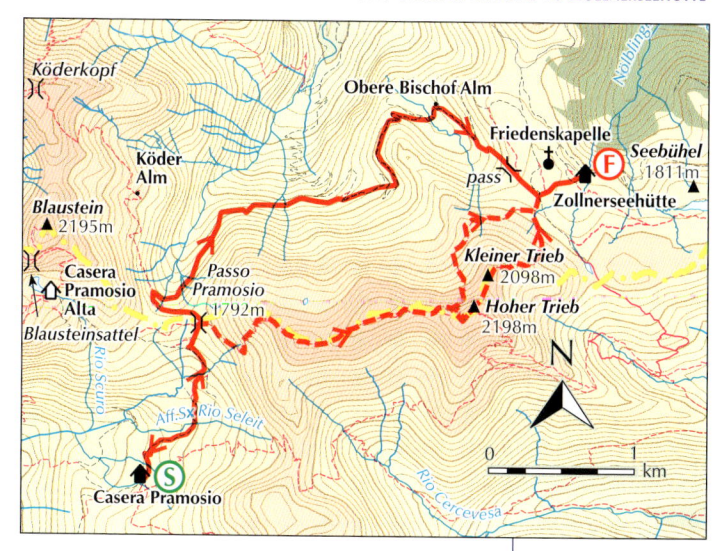

STAGE 5C – ITALIAN ROUTE: CASERA PRAMOSIO TO ZOLLNERSEEHÜTTE

The **Friedenskapelle**, the Peace Chapel, located next door to the hut, was built in the 1980s to commemorate fallen soldiers of World War I, some of whom are interred here.

Hoher Trieb variant – challenging

From the Passo Pramosio, it takes about 2hr to get to the Zollnerseehütte along the main Karnischer Höhenweg or 3hr 15min if you take the high route and climb over Hoher Trieb (2198m). The walk up is relatively straightforward, with great views and more interesting trenchworks, this time Italian. There are two ways down from Hoher Trieb and both are challenging. They can be avoided by retracing your steps to the Passo Pramosio to join the main Karnischer Höhenweg.

From the Passo Pramosio, head south-east along the 448, climbing across open moor. As the path swings north-east, the climb gets steeper before levelling and swinging east along an old military road behind a ridge and extensive trenchworks. Just before the summit itself,

THE KARNISCHER HÖHENWEG

On top of Hoher Trieb

To avoid both descents, consider returning via the ascent route, descending to the Passo Pramosio and joining the main route.

there are some old barracks. Cables are positioned to support the final few steps to the summit of **Hoher Trieb**.

There are two routes down, both marked 421. The most direct route heads north-east from the summit to **Kleiner Trieb** (2098m): it looks intimidating and involves cables. For the other route, head west from the summit, retracing your steps for a short distance, before heading north and then descending a very steep grassy bank on the western side, which is also challenging. ◀ Both descents join the main Karnischer Höhenweg south-east of the unnamed pass (towards the end of the main route), then head north-east for 250 metres to the **Zollnerseehütte**.

STAGE 6
Zollnerseehütte to Nassfeld

Start	Zollnerseehütte
Distance	23.8km
Ascent/Descent	970m/1080m
Difficulty	Moderate
Walking time	8hr 20min
Maximum altitude	2030m
Refreshments	Straniger Alm, 2hr from the start
Routefinding	Good waymarking: follow the 403

Stage 6 is a long, relatively gentle day that follows a route through a range of different landscapes, some familiar, some new. Although the alpine scenery of the first five days is still there to be enjoyed, a pastoral landscape, the landscape that will dominate the last two stages of the walk, starts to emerge. Here, the dominant features are rich meadows, farmsteads and cattle. There are still some big mountains to appreciate, however, and the best one, Trogkofel (2279m), comes towards the day's end.

The final part of the walk involves a knee-crunching descent into Nassfeld, a ski resort located above a pass. The noisiness of the resort provides a sharp, unwelcome contrast to what is otherwise quite a remote walk. The best views are those to the south and east, where the distinct Dolomite-like silhouette of the Julian Alps is a constant distraction.

The World War I front line and Karnischer Höhenweg diverge on this stretch of the route, with the front line heading south-east (to the deadly Isonzo front) near Trogkofel. The route continues to follow the border, however, which reflects the gains Italy made at the end of World War I.

ALTERNATIVE SCHEDULES

If 8hr 20min is too long, consider staying longer at the Zollnerseehütte and breaking the day up by walking to the Straniger Alm (2hr from the Zollnerseehütte). Local walking opportunities include the ascent of Hoher

THE KARNISCHER HÖHENWEG

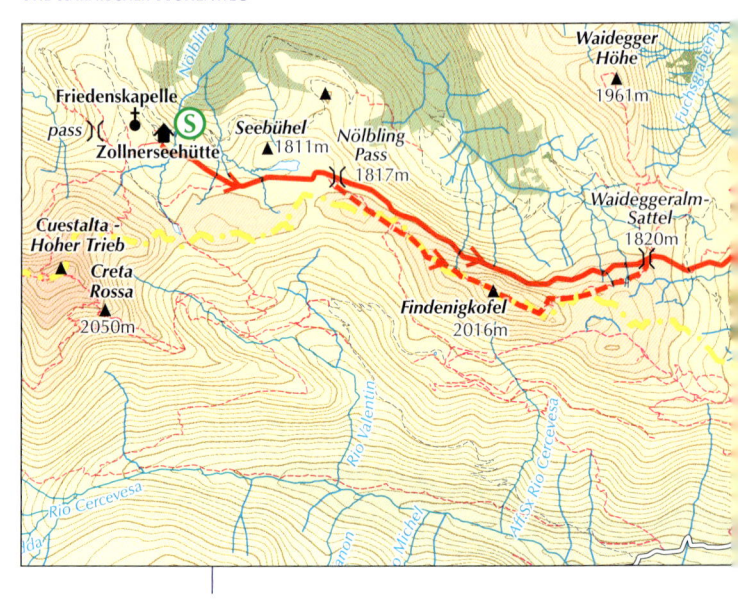

Trieb (2hr 15min from the Zollnerseehütte, retracing one of the descent routes from Hoher Trieb or Kleiner Trieb described in Stage 5C) or walking around the Zollnersee Geotrail.

There are also particularly good options here for leaving the Karnischer Höhenweg altogether. It is possible to walk down to train stations to the north of the route in about 2hr 30min from either the Zollnerseehütte or Straniger Alm. Alternatively, towards the end of the stage, instead of staying at Nassfeld, you could take the Millennium Express cable car at the Madritsche Ski Station and again catch the train to Villach in the valley below.

Head south-east from the Zollnerseehütte following a gently climbing path across what can be a boggy meadow. After 900 metres, a shallow little lake, the Zollnersee, is reached and the path passes it on its southern side.

Stage 6 – Zollnerseehütte to Nassfeld

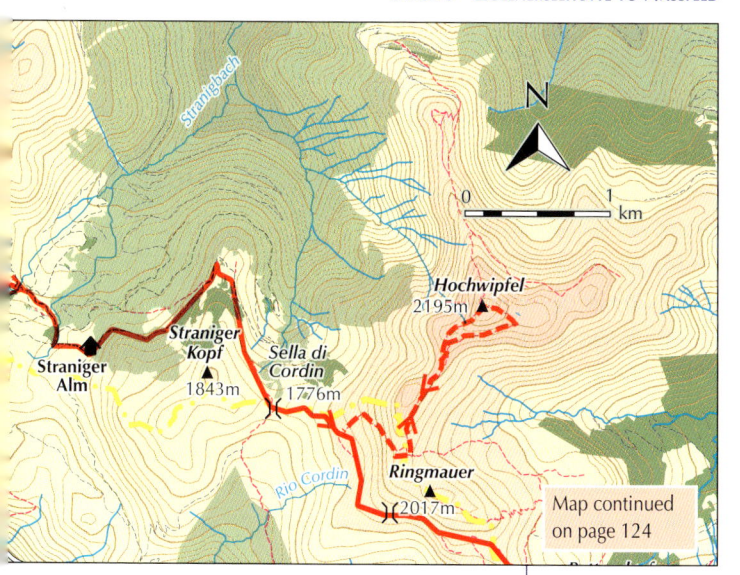

Ignore a junction and right-hand turn just beyond the lake and continue along the 403 up to the **Nölbling Pass** (1817m). ▶ From the pass, follow a contouring path, narrow in places, for 2km along the northern flank of Findenigkofel to the **Waideggeralm-Sattel** (1820m).

| To go via Findenigkofel (see variant below), turn right just after the pass.

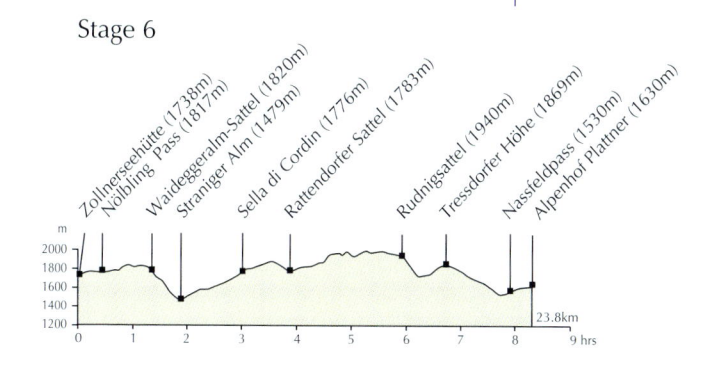

Stage 6

121

The Karnischer Höhenweg

Looking towards the Zollnersee from the Nölbling Pass

The lovely contouring path from the Nölbling Pass, another military supply route, is called the **Hennebergweg**. It is named after General Major Henneberg, who was killed near the pass in an avalanche.

Just beyond the pass, you should get your first view of the Julian Alps. There are also great views across the valley: opposite is the Waidegger Höhe (1961m), and the farmstead nestling on a shoulder beneath it is called the Waidegger Alm.

Findenigkofel variant – moderate

Turn right just after the Nölbling Pass and follow the 425 up **Findenigkofel** (2016m). After visiting the summit, the route heads east to rejoin the main route at the **Waideggeralm-Sattel**.

This is a pleasant walk, visiting more trenchworks. It takes about 40min more than the main route and involves another 200m of climb along what is effectively a ridge.

From the Waideggeralm-Sattel, follow the path down through meadows to the **Straniger Alm** (1479m). The path through the hillside meadows may be overgrown, and the waymarks, sometimes marked on little poles that are not always upright, hard to spot. The Alm, however, should soon be visible at the bottom of the valley on a dirt road.

STAGE 6 – ZOLLNERSEEHÜTTE TO NASSFELD

The **Straniger Alm** (mob +43 (0)680 2220262 **www.straniger-alm.at**) is a working farm that provides food together with both individual rooms and dormitory-style accommodation. The food is excellent and includes all the highlights of Gailtal cuisine.

GAILTAL CUISINE

Cheesemaking – heating the milk in a vat

The Gailtal valley and the Nassfeld region are proud of their mountain cuisine. The most important products are dried bacon (*Gailtaler Speck*), smoked salmon (*Gailtaler Räucherlachs*) and cheese (*Gailtaler Almkäse*).

The cheese is particularly important and its name has been awarded protected status by the European Union. There are only 14 accredited producers and the Straniger Alm is one of them. The cheese is produced on a cooperative basis, with the master cheesemaker, the herdsman or herdswoman and the owner of each cow all taking a share of the produce. It must be made from raw alpine cow's milk, although in certain cases raw goat's milk can be added up to a maximum of 10 per cent. The milk used must be produced from designated pastures and processed in designated dairies.

The cows are milked twice a day, with the evening milk cooled and set aside to mature overnight in round wooden containers called *Stotzen*. In the morning, it is placed in a vat and combined with fresh morning milk. It is heated to 32°C and inoculated with rennet. The curdled milk is then cut into lentil-sized pieces. The curds are heated, put into moulds for approximately two days and then pressed slowly. The freshly produced cheese is brine-salted for two to three days in order to develop a natural rind. Finally, it is set aside to age for a minimum of seven weeks in a ripening room.

Hiking and cheese enthusiasts can combine their passions by walking the 32km Käsewanderweg (cheese trail), tasting and comparing products from 13 of the 14 producers.

The Karnischer Höhenweg

Follow the dirt road past the Straniger Alm and gently up the valley side for 600 metres. As the road turns south, leave it, pass through a gate and join a forest road heading north-north-east through trees. Continue climbing on the road for 600 metres as it works its way around the **Straniger Kopf** (1843m). The route then leaves the forest road, joins a path and heads south on the eastern side of the mountain.

After about 1km, a pass, the **Sella di Cordin** (1776m), is reached and the 403 returns to Italy. The pine trees that have dominated the climb since the Straniger Alm are now left behind and the route once again enters a classic limestone terrain populated by low rhododendron shrubs and alder bushes.

From the pass, the route swings east (ignoring paths heading south-west) and continues to climb gently along the Italian border. After 400 metres, as the path swings south-east, a junction provides the option of a circular walk up to the top of Hochwipfel (2195m).

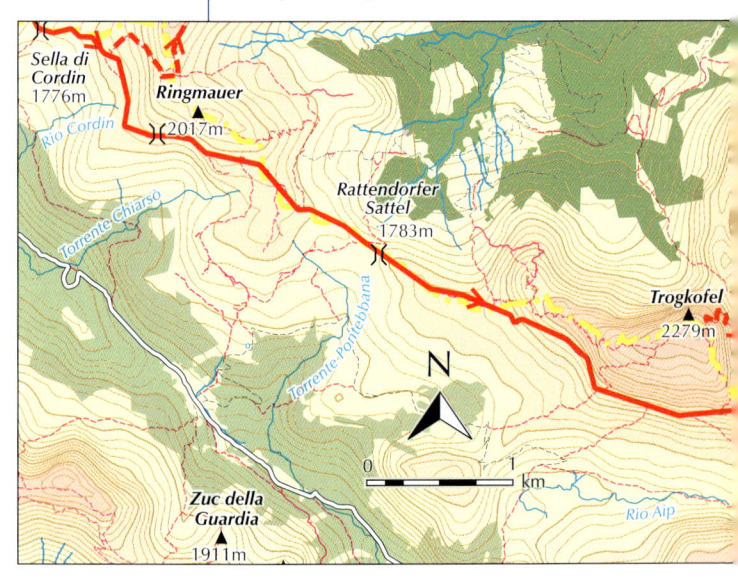

Stage 6 – Zollnerseehütte to Nassfeld

Optional ascent of Hochwipfel – moderate

From the junction it is a 400m climb along an easy grassy path (the 419 and the 417) to the summit of **Hochwipfel**. Depending on weather and schedule, this is an excellent place for a lunch stop. The route does a circuit of the summit before retracing steps to the main path. The round trip takes about 2hr.

Continue south and then east, climbing through increasingly rocky terrain to an unnamed **pass**. The views from the pass are excellent. Immediately to the north are the cliffs of **Ringmauer** (2017m), named because of its resemblance to a coliseum, ahead of the magnificent Trogkofel (2279m), and beyond that, to the south-east, the Julian Alps.

Follow the path down and across a wide saddle, the **Rattendorfer Sattel** (1783m), with the terrain now falling gently away to the north and south. Long trenchworks running parallel with the border, clearly marked with

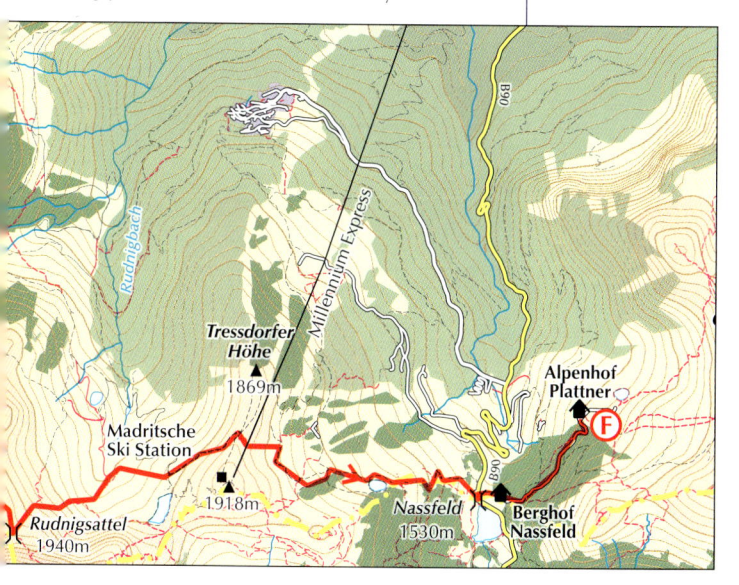

THE KARNISCHER HÖHENWEG

the ever-present white border stones, mark the way. The ground at the saddle is boggy, peaty and wet, and the area is famous for its sinkholes.

Continue east from the saddle for about 100 metres and clamber up a rocky outcrop. ◄ Once on top of the rocks, continue climbing, now at a more even pace, up to a signpost marking the junction with the 419. Continue east, traversing a scree field immediately underneath the cliffs of Trogkofel. Follow a well-defined and easy path for about 1km to a junction with the 413, which is the best place to start a climb up to Trogkofel (see variant below).

These rocks (hollowed out for World War I gun emplacements) dominate the otherwise flat terrain to the west.

> Standing slightly apart and with huge vertical cliffs, **Trogkofel** is one of the most beautiful mountains in the Carnic Alps. At 2279m, it is the second highest

Border post at the Rattendorfer Sattel, with Trogkofel in the background

mountain east of the Plöckenpass, after Polinik (2332m), but looking like a fortress it is far more striking. Of particular interest is its relatively flat top, the size of a football field, with its classic dry limestone landscape of little islands of vegetation dotted around the crevices. Sustaining the Carnic theme of geological complexity, the limestone on the plateau is unique, early Permian, and with its own designation – Trogkofel limestone.

Trogkofel variant – challenging
Trogkofel is very popular with climbers but there is one route, known as the south-west route, which is suitable for experienced hikers. From the junction, head north along the 413 to the main rock face. Climb up through a ravine/chimney via a series of ladders and pins driven into the rock, before emerging onto the plateau. Return to the junction by the same route. The Trogkofel variant will take just over 2hr.

From the junction with the 413, follow the path for 1km to the end of the valley, the Trogkofelsattel (2030m), and then swing south-east and head along a ridge to the next pass, the **Rudnigsattel** (1940m), where there is a very conspicuous bivouac immediately to the right. The ridge forms the boundary between a quiet, empty world and one full of ski lifts – the route now has to cross the ski resort of Nassfeld.

From the Rudnigsattel, follow the 403 east along a descending path into trees. The path is rocky and progress frustratingly slow. Continue for about 800 metres (descending 200m) and, ignoring a junction with the 413, cross a stream. Continue east for 1km and climb up to a ridge, the **Tressdorfer Höhe** (1869m).

> The **Madritsche Ski Station** is located up along the ridge to the south and it's from here that the Millennium Express cable car disgorges visitors who have made the journey up from the valley below. Local summer attractions include a Wild

West theme park, an aqua park and a toboggan run (the Pendolino). The cable car provides a good way of getting off the main ridge if the plan is to finish the walk early. It takes about 20min to get down by cable car to Tröpolach, and from the ski station in the town it's another 20min walk to Tröpolach railway station across the valley, for trains to Villach.

From the ridge, continue along the 403 and head down into the valley. The path crosses a bridge over the toboggan run and passes underneath the cable car, and then heads through trees and down a ski run to the pass below. After descending for 300m over a distance of 2km, the route reaches the main road over the **Nassfeldpass** (1530m), where there is a bar and a hotel. If staying at the **Alpenhof Plattner** (1630m), cross the main road and follow a side road up the hill on the other side of the valley for 900 metres.

> There are two hotels directly on the route. The first is the **Berghof Nassfeld** (tel +43 (0)4285 8271 www.berghof.or.at) immediately next to the road and the pass itself. Although adequate, the hotel lacks personality, and most Karnischer Höhenweg walkers stay at the **Alpenhof Plattner** (tel +43 (0)4285 8285 www.plattner.at), which is slightly less of a 'ski resort' hotel and offers a discount for Alpine Club members.

STAGE 7
Nassfeld to Gasthaus Starhand

Start	Alpenhof Plattner, Nassfeld
Distance	26.6km
Ascent/Descent	1100m/1270m
Difficulty	Easy
Walking time	8hr 20min
Maximum altitude	1885m
Refreshments	Garnitzenalm, Eggeralm
Routefinding	Well marked. Follow the 403 all the way, apart from the long route around the valley just after Dellacher Alm, which is not the 403. (The optional shortcut across the valley is the 403.)

Stage 7 is a long but otherwise easy day. There are two ridges that have to be crossed, one at the beginning and one near the end, and the walking between them is fairly flat. After escaping the ski resort at Nassfeld, the route follows a trail along a valley through a forest before emerging into beautiful meadows around Eggeralm, which in the summer will be full of cattle. It then follows a forest road around a valley before climbing through meadows, over a ridge and down to another tiny transhumance settlement at Starhand.

ALTERNATIVE SCHEDULES

If 8hr 20min is too long, the stage can be split in half by staying at Eggeralm.

The second half of the route has in the past been the victim of storm damage. The route described takes the long way around a valley, and about 1hr could be saved if the 403 is followed all the way. However, the 403 involves a difficult rope-assisted path across a gully; if the path is no longer viable, then it may be necessary to return to the described route and follow the more indirect path.

THE KARNISCHER HÖHENWEG

Taking an extra day to get to Starhand makes it possible to make an easy climb up to Gartnerkofel (2195m), which is immediately above the Alpenhof Plattner, or, on the second day, to climb Poludnig (1999m).

Another possibility, if you want to climb Oisternig (2052m), is to continue beyond the Gasthaus Starhand to the Gasthaus Oisternig in Feistritzer Alm (1hr), spend the night there and climb Oisternig before embarking on Stage 8: see route directions in Stage 8.

The Gasthaus Starhand is nice but very primitive. Alternative accommodation used to be available at the Rifugio Nordio Deffar, just beyond the Gasthaus Starhand, across the border in Italy. Unfortunately, the Rifugio was damaged by a fire in early 2016 and at the time of writing is closed.

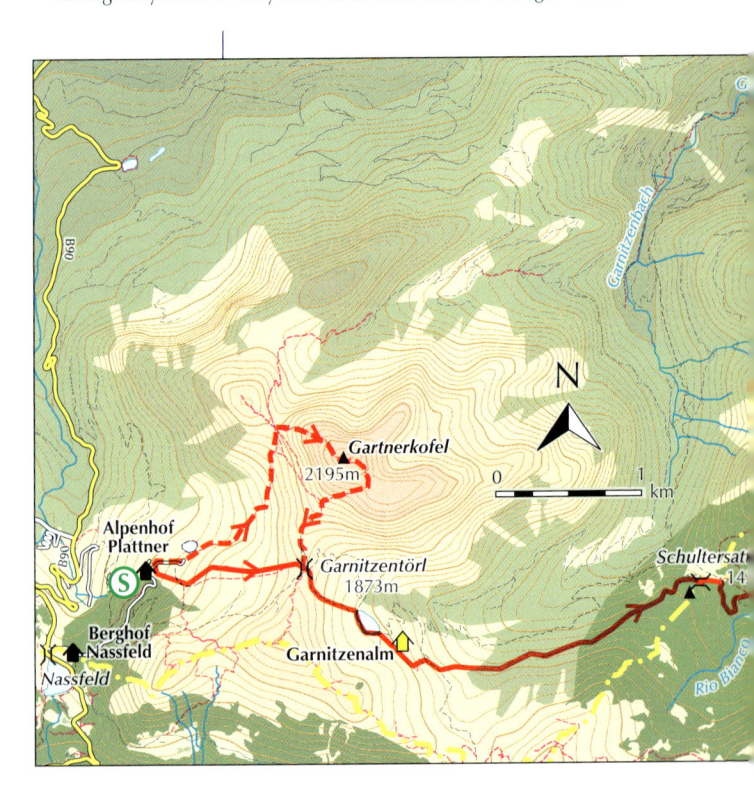

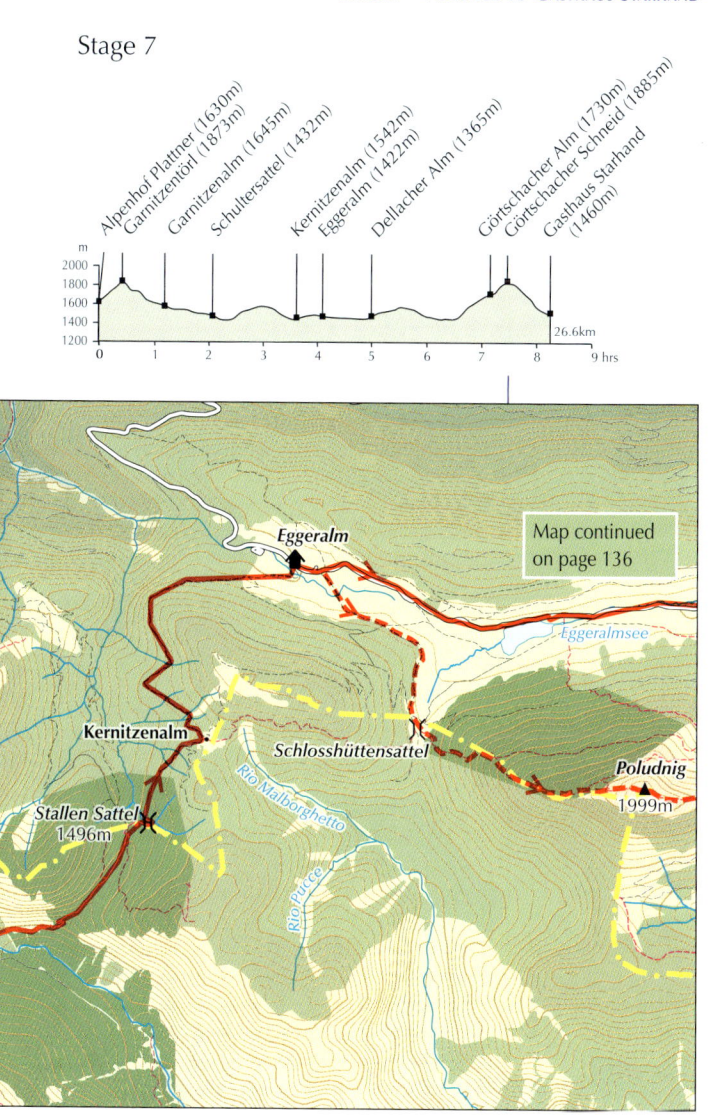

Stage 7 – Nassfeld to Gasthaus Starhand

Stage 7

Alpenhof Plattner (1630m)
Garnitzentörl (1873m)
Garnitzenalm (1645m)
Schultersattel (1432m)
Kernitzenalm (1542m)
Eggeralm (1422m)
Dellacher Alm (1365m)
Görtschacher Alm (1730m)
Görtschacher Schneid (1885m)
Gasthaus Starhand (1460m)

26.6km

Map continued on page 136

THE KARNISCHER HÖHENWEG

From the Alpenhof Plattner, cross the road and follow a path climbing east across open ground. The path swings to the north-east into larch trees, crosses a stream and continues a relentless 200m and 45min climb alongside a piste up to the **Garnitzentörl** pass (1873m).

> The strictly protected **Wulfenia** (*Wulfenia carinthiaca*) is a violet-blue flower that, along with its even rarer white-flowering variant (*Wulfenia carinthiaca alba*), is unique to Carinthia and grows at the foot of Gartnerkofel. It is named after its discoverer, Franz Xaver Freiherr von Wulfen, who found it over 220 years ago.

Gartnerkofel variant – moderate
Gartnerkofel (2195m) is an easy climb and in good weather provides an excellent place to see the Julian Alps to the south-east and, to the north, the Hohe Tauern and the Großglockner, Großvenediger and Hochalmspitze. This variant adds 2hr to the schedule.

Gartnerkofel from near Garnitzenalm

STAGE 7 – NASSFELD TO GASTHAUS STARHAND

From Alpenhof Plattner, follow the road up to the Watschiger Alm and join the 410 heading across meadows to the Kühweger Törl, and then the 412 across to **Gartnerkofel**, marked with a large Carinthian cross. From here, head south-west down to the top of a chairlift and then down to the **Garnitzentörl**.

From the pass, follow a well-defined trail through pine trees along the southern side of the valley – still part of the ski resort. To the north are the vertical limestone cliffs of Gartnerkofel. After a steep 120m descent, pass to the right-hand side of a **reservoir** and continue to the **Garnitzenalm** (1645m). ▸

> If it's not too early, the Garnitzenalm should be open for coffee.

Follow the dirt road east from the Garnitzenalm for 100 metres and then join a path that heads across a meadow into trees. Descend to a stream, cross it and join a forest road. After 1.6km, the forest road reaches a barely perceptible pass, the **Schultersattel** (1432m) and crosses the border from Austria to Italy. ▸

> If the weather is good, views through gaps in the larch trees provide the final views of the Hohe Tauern to the north-west.

Continue along the dirt road for 300 metres (it heads south before swinging north) and then leave it to join a path heading east. Running along a valley, and parallel with a stream below, the path follows the remains of an old military road that is gradually succumbing to gravity and the effects of nature. In places, streams running down the valley side have washed the road away, and steel ropes and chains have been positioned to help cross the watery obstacles. The path swings north-east and climbs gently into a gully running into the main valley and up to the **Stallen Sattel** (1496m).

Now back in Austria, continue on the path for 200 metres to a forest road. The forest road descends and ascends around a little gully and then continues in the same direction, north-east. After 600 metres of fairly level walking, you reach a meadow with a little farmstead, the **Kernitzenalm** (1542m). ▸

> The border with Italy is at the top of the meadow to the right.

Continue along the dirt road for 2.3km to where it opens up (now heading east) into a wide and lush valley. In the middle of the valley, 300 metres ahead, is **Eggeralm** (1422m).

Eggeralm is a small compact village consisting of 40 or so identical wooden chalets. They are now mostly holiday homes but traditionally the chalets were summer homes for the milkmaids who looked after the brown-and-white cows that still feature in the nearby fields. The **Gasthaus zum Rudi** (mob +43 (0)676 9343605 www.zumrudi.at) provides both excellent food and a limited amount of comfortable accommodation.

Poludnig variant – moderate

If the stage has been divided into two with a stay at Eggeralm, then the easy walk up to Poludnig (1999m) should be considered. It adds an extra 90min to the second part of the stage but avoids a stretch of road walking and provides more great views of the Hohe Tauern and the Julian Alps.

At the junction in the centre of Eggeralm, follow the route marked 483 south-east to **Schlosshüttensattel**, then on to **Poludnig**, before rejoining the main route via **Poludniger Alm** (a small summer hamlet with refreshments).

Eggeralm and its cheesemakers

Stage 7 – Nassfeld to Gasthaus Starhand

Main route

Leaving Eggeralm, continue east along the road through meadows (full of grazing cows when I was there) for 1.5km down to the **Eggeralmsee**, a wide shallow lake in the bottom of the valley. ▶ From the lake, continue along the road for 2km to **Dellacher Alm** (1365m), a smaller version of Eggeralm. The route does not actually enter the hamlet but leaves the road and climbs along a well-defined path heading south-east across a meadow and up into trees. After crossing another trail, it follows what is now a forest road that switchbacks its way south up the mountainside. At the second switchback, it reaches the junction with the 483, the path heading down from Poludnig.

Continue south along the road for 500 metres to where the 403 leaves the forest road. At this point there is a choice: either stick to the scheduled long way round the valley or follow the potentially difficult path 403 across the valley.

If you're carrying a picnic, this is the perfect place to stop.

Shortcut across valley – potentially challenging

From the forest road, path 403 heads down through trees and cuts directly across the valley, which could save 1hr on the scheduled route. However, it involves crossing an unstable ravine, where ropes have been positioned to help. The route may change from year to year and could be challenging.

Assuming a cautious approach is adopted, ignore the 403 and continue south-west along the forest road. After 1km, turn left at a junction, leave a popular mountain bike trail that continues up to Poludnig, and head down the valley, still following the forest road. Descending along a switchback road, the route leaves the trees and once again encounters meadows. After 2.5km it reaches the bottom of the valley, crosses a stream and, now on the other side of the valley, heads north-east. Signs warn of bears!

Continue north for 1km to where a side valley is reached. ▶ Just after crossing a stream, turn right and follow the 403 along a dirt road heading directly up

Here is the junction with the original 403, a more direct route.

135

The Karnischer Höhenweg

> If you have spare energy, turn left and follow a path to Starhand summit (1965m), then retrace your steps to the main route (a 30min detour).

the side valley. After 300 metres, the 403 **leaves the dirt road** (which now turns north-west), heads into trees and climbs steeply up the side of the valley before once again rejoining the dirt road, which has taken a longer route. Continue along the dirt road through meadows into the little settlement of **Görtschacher Alm** (1730m). After passing the wooden chalets of the hamlet, follow a path across a meadow and climb up to the pass, the **Görtschacher Schneid** (1885m). ◄

From the pass, continue south across a meadow for about 200 metres, swing north into trees and then head east and down to a dispersed transhumance village, the **Dolinza Alm**, in the centre of which is the **Gasthaus Starhand** (1460m).

> The **Gasthaus Starhand** (tel +43 (0)4283 2004, mob +43 (0)664 9470231) is charming and friendly, but primitive. Accommodation is provided in a single dormitory and washing facilities are limited. The food, however, is hearty and excellent. It

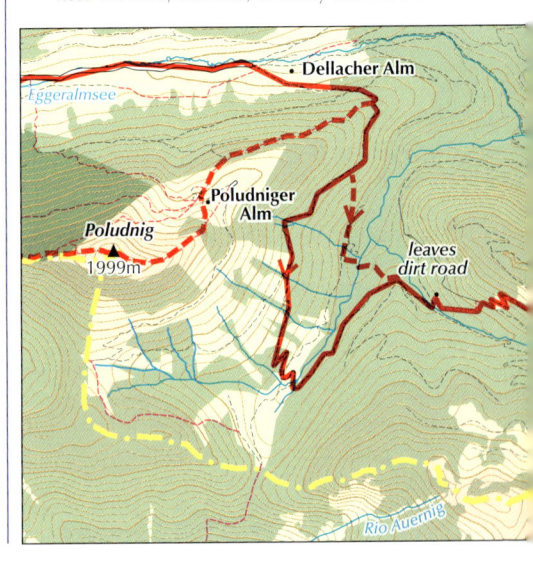

Stage 7 – Nassfeld to Gasthaus Starhand

THE GREAT BEAR COMEBACK

The European brown bear, at a potential 300kg, is by far Europe's biggest natural predator and is making a tentative comeback in central Europe. Most of the 14,000 population live in Russia, Romania and the Balkans, but they have also continued to thrive in Slovenia. With the fall of the Iron Curtain, some of these bears started to move west and their numbers have been enhanced by resettlement projects in Italy, France and Austria. Actual sightings, however, are incredibly rare and only a handful of bears have actually been born in Carinthia. The attitude of the local farmers is distinctly mixed, and illegal shooting has hampered the success of resettlement projects. Despite this, the advertised bear sausages and bear burgers do not contain the real thing.

is not usually busy but may not open unless it has bookings.

The potential alternative to Gasthaus Starhand is the **Rifugio Nordio Deffar**, which at the time of writing is closed as a consequence of fire damage.

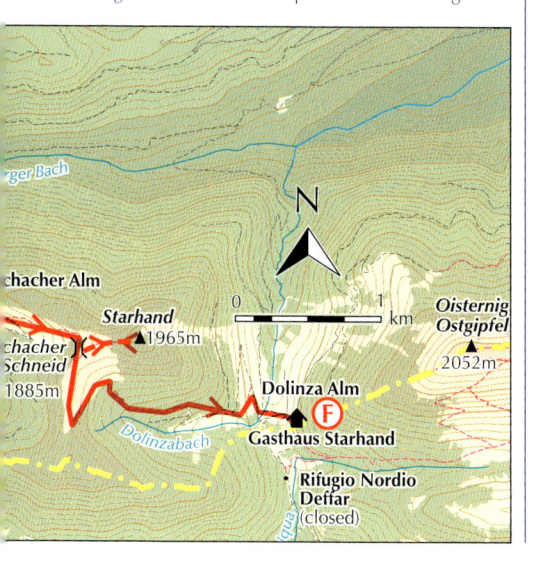

Accommodation at Gasthof Starhand

If it has reopened, it can be found by heading south past the Gasthaus Starhand on the 403 along a path that climbs gently into trees. After 100 metres, the path crosses the border into Italy and reaches a junction. Turn left and head down the valley (on the Italian 507). The Rifugio is reached after 200 metres.

STAGE 8
Gasthaus Starhand to Arnoldstein

Start	Gasthaus Starhand
Distance	28km to Arnoldstein (23km to Thörl-Maglern)
Ascent/Descent	1100m/1800m
Difficulty	Moderate
Walking time	8hr 30min to Arnoldstein (7hr 30min to Thörl-Maglern)
Maximum altitude	1722m
Refreshments	Possibilities at Feistritzer Alm, Achomitzer Alm and Thörl-Maglern
Routefinding	Well marked, but logging can provide some challenges. Follow the 403 all the way to Thörl-Maglern.

Stage 8, the last stage on the Karnischer Höhenweg, involves a long and sometimes tough walk, mainly through conifer and beech forest. Although descents are its dominant characteristic, there is still some climbing to do before finishing the end-to-end walk of the Carnic Alps.

The Karnischer Höhenweg 'officially' ends at Thörl-Maglern, the small town that sits in the pass between the Carnic Alps and the next range, the Karavanke, but our route continues to Arnoldstein. Although there are bus and rail transport options from Thörl-Maglern to Arnoldstein, the service is infrequent, so although 5km of flat walking is a distinctively anti-climatic way to finish an epic mountain walk, it is the most reliable option.

From the Gasthaus Starhand, head south on the 403 and climb gently into trees. After 100 metres, the path crosses the border with Italy and reaches a junction with a path (the Italian 507) heading down to the Rifugio Nordio Deffar. Ignore the turn-off and stay on the 403 as it swings east and continues its climb through trees. After 200 metres, the path reaches a second junction with the 507 – this is the more direct return route from the Rifugio.

Continue climbing up a valley, emerging eventually into meadows and reaching the summer settlement

THE KARNISCHER HÖHENWEG

Leaving Feistritzer Alm — of **Feistritzer Alm** (1722m) about 1hr after leaving the Gasthaus Starhand.

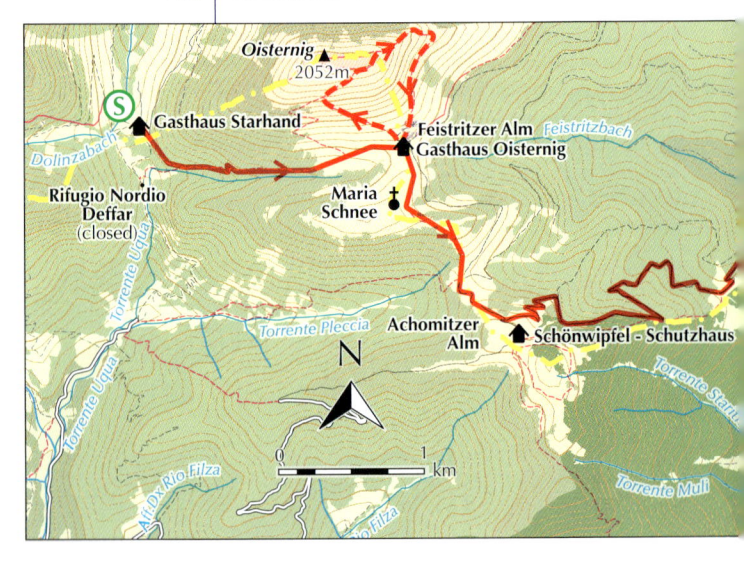

STAGE 8 – GASTHAUS STARHAND TO ARNOLDSTEIN

Stage 8

Gasthaus Starhand (1460m)
Feistritzer Alm (1722m)
Achomitzer Alm (1715m)
Bartolo-Sattel (1175m)
saddle (1685m)
Göriacher Alm (1644m)
birdwatching tower (1340m)
Thörl-Maglern (690m)
Arnoldstein (578m)

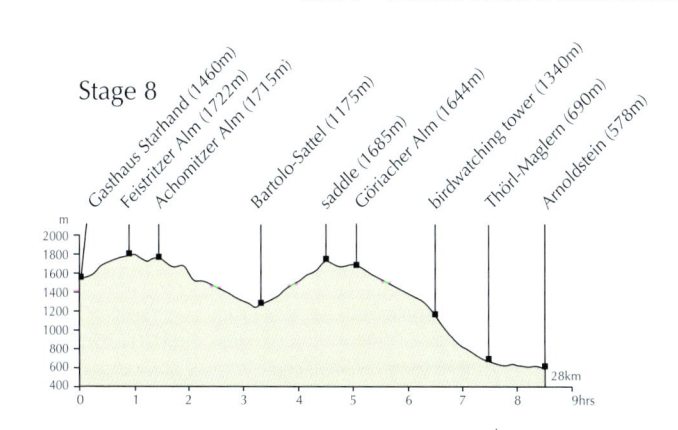

Gasthaus Oisternig (mob +43 (0)699 17242520) in Feistritzer Alm provides both food and primitive accommodation (similar to but slightly more primitive than the Gasthaus Starhand).

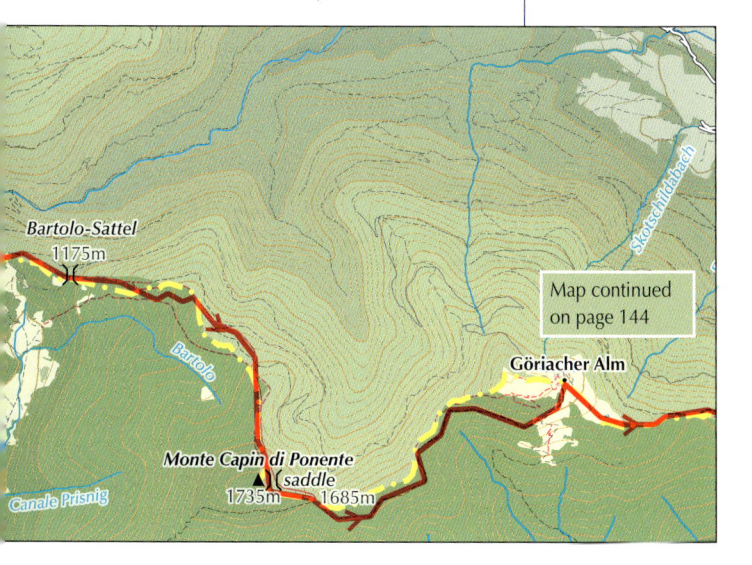

Map continued on page 144

The Karnischer Höhenweg

Optional ascent of Oisternig – easy
If you have stayed overnight at the Gasthaus Oisternig, consider the easy climb to the little summit immediately to the north, Oisternig (2052m). From Feistritzer Alm, head north-west along the 481, zigzagging to **Oisternig** summit. It will take about an hour. Head along the ridge to the cross and follow a path heading initially north-east (now the 482), before swinging south and returning to the **Feistritzer Alm**.

Head south from Feistritzer Alm, climbing gently up to a tiny but beautiful hill-top chapel, the **Maria Schnee**. From the church, continue south across a shallow grassy valley to another little settlement, the **Achomitzer Alm** (1715m).

In the Achomitzer Alm (a 5min detour from the main route), there is a private refuge, the **Schönwipfel-Schutzhaus** (mob +43 (0)664 11410579), which provides both food and accommodation.

Continue on the main route, following a forest road that switchbacks its way down the side of the valley. After 3km, leave it and turn right onto a path, heading through trees. Follow the path for 1km to the **Bartolo-Sattel** (1175m). ◄ Crossing the forest road, follow a path into beech trees on what is a long and seemingly relentless ascent. After 40min, join a forest road and follow it for 400 metres to where it rejoins a path – if you're distracted, the turn-off is easily missed. The route now traverses the steep eastern flank of **Monte Capin di Ponente** (1735m), where the terrain is falling away to the east and in places has to be navigated with care. After another 300 metres, waymarks on a rock point east and announce that the top of a **saddle** (1685m) has been reached. ◄ Soon after, the path joins a forest road.

Head east and follow a level road for 2.8km to the **Göriacher Alm** (1644m), a scattered group of wooden chalets in the middle of open ground. The Göriacher Alm marks the start of a 1000m descent and the beginning of the end of the Carnic ridge. Turn left at a sign

A sign at the Bartolo-Sattel tells you it's another 4hr 15min to Thörl-Maglern.

Monte Capin itself is not climbed.

STAGE 8 – GASTHAUS STARHAND TO ARNOLDSTEIN

The long climb up to the saddle below Monte Capin di Ponente

positioned just to the east of the Göriacher Alm. ▶ Head down across a meadow, pass between two small lakes and head into trees. Continue for just under 2km, along a mix of forest paths and roads and following ever-present border markings. The route then turns abruptly left. If you end up at a **birdwatching tower** (1340m) – easily done – you've gone a little too far and will need to retrace your steps.

From the turn before the birdwatching tower, the descent gets significantly steeper and follows a path through conifers and birches down the mountainside. On the way, it crosses a forest road that takes a more gradual descent. Forestry work may obscure the path in places but generally speaking it is well waymarked. After a 500m descent, the waymarks lead to a forest road.

The sign tells you that Thörl-Maglern is 2hr away.

The Karnischer Höhenweg

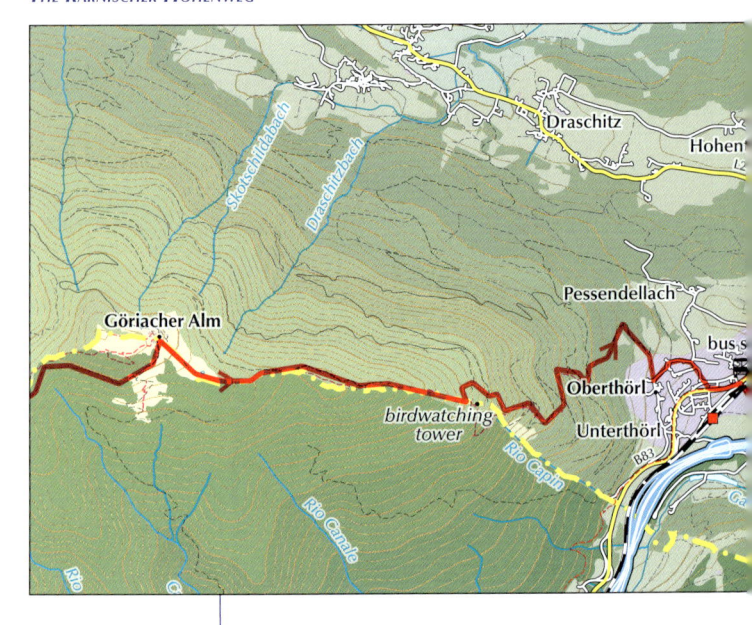

Oberthörl (Upper Thörl), along with Unterthörl (Lower Thörl), is part of **Thörl-Maglern**, the 'official' end to the Karnischer Höhenweg.

Follow the road as it emerges from the trees, crosses a meadow and heads into the village of **Oberthörl** (690m). Continue through the village to a roadside bar (the Mikl Bar) and a **bus stop**. ◄ The bus service is not frequent, and the train service (from the railway station, some 200 metres to the right on the other side of the road) is even less frequent. Unless you're very lucky with the times, walking to Arnoldstein, involving 5km of flat walking, is the best option.

From the bus stop, head south for a few metres, turn left, take a bridge over the railway line and follow a local road, swinging east towards houses. Turn left at the houses and follow route 3 north and back towards the railway line. Continue along route 3, following a quiet road through a mix of fields and houses for 2km, where the route leaves the road and continues along a track. Follow the track as it heads down to the River Gailitz and underneath a motorway. After 1.2km, the route turns left

Stage 8 – Gasthaus Starhand to Arnoldstein

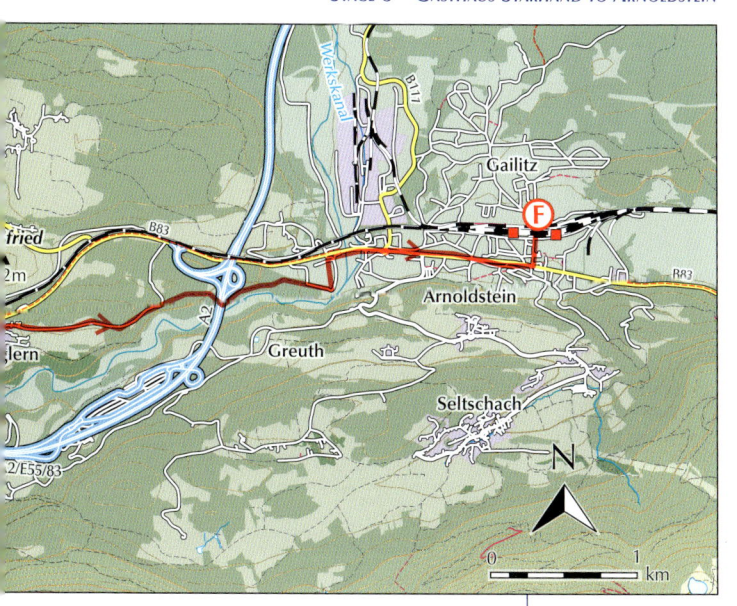

and heads up to the road. Turn right at the road and follow it into the centre of **Arnoldstein** (578m).

Arnoldstein is just to the north of the point where the borders of Austria, Italy and Slovenia meet. Although the town has accommodation, its best feature for current purposes is the railway station, from where there is a frequent service to Villach and onwards to various international airports.

If you decide to stay in Arnoldstein (although Villach is a more interesting place), the nicest hotel, close to the station, is the **Hotel und Genusswirt Wallner** (tel +43 (0)4255 2356).

APPENDIX A
Route breakdown

Key waypoints	Accommodation	Time (non-cumulative)	Time (cumulative)	Distance (km)
Stage 1: Arnbach to Obstanserseehütte			**8hr 45min**	18.3
Alpenhotel Weitlanbrunn (1100m)	✓			
junction with Helmweg (1698m)		2hr	2hr	
border (2342m)		2hr	4hr	
Sillianer Hütte (2447m)	✓	30min	4hr 30min	
Obermahdsattel (2470m)		10min	4hr 40min	
Hochgränten Pass (2429m)		1hr 15min	5hr 55min	
Eisenreich (2665m)		2hr	7hr 55min	
Obstanserseehütte (2304m)	✓	50min	8hr 45min	
Stage 2: Obstanserseehütte to Porzehütte			**6hr 30min**	12.2
Obstanserseehütte (2304m)	✓			
Sella Frugnoni (2539m)		40min	40min	
Obstanser Sattel (2453m)		20min	1hr	
2587m junction		15min	1hr 15min	
Pfannspitze (2678m)		25min	1hr 40min	

APPENDIX A – ROUTE BREAKDOWN

Key waypoints	Accommodation	Time (non-cumulative)	Time (cumulative)	Distance (km)
Kinigatscharte (2515m)		1hr	2hr 40min	
Hintersattel (2520m)		40min	3hr 20min	
Standschützenhütte (2350m)	✓	20min	3hr 40min	
Oberer Stuckensee (2032m)		30min	4hr 10min	
Heretalm (2170m)		45min	4hr 55min	
power lines (2181m)		25min	5hr 20min	
Porzehütte (1942m)	✓	1hr 10min	6hr 30min	
Stage 3: Porzehütte to Hochweißsteinhaus			**8hr**	**17.8**
Porzehütte (1942m)	✓			
Tilliacher Joch (2094m)		20min	20min	
Bärenbadegg (2431m)		1hr	1hr 20min	
Kesselscharte (2293m)		40min	2hr	
Winklerjoch (2250m)		1hr	3hr	
Forcella Val Mezzana (2268m)		30min	3hr 30min	
Hochspitzjoch (2314m)		20min	3hr 50min	
saddle (2450m)		1hr	4hr 50min	
Steinkarspitze (2524m)		40min	5hr 30min	
Luggauer Sattel (2404m)		1hr	6hr 30min	

The Karnischer Höhenweg

Key waypoints	Accommodation	Time (non-cumulative)	Time (cumulative)	Distance (km)
Luggauer Törl (2232m)		30min	7hr	
Hochweißsteinhaus (1867m)	✓	1hr	8hr	
Stage 4: Hochweißsteinhaus to Gasthof Valentinalm			**9hr**	**23.2**
Hochweißsteinhaus (1867m)	✓			
Öfner Joch (2011m)		20min	20min	
Casera Fleons di Sopra (1862m)		10min	30min	
Casera Fleons di Sotto (1576m)		50min	1hr 20min	
Casera Sissanis di Sotto (1684m)		40min	2hr	
Sella Sissanis (1987m)		1hr 15min	3hr 15min	
Passo di Niedergail (1994m)		20min	3hr 35min	
Giramondopass (2005m)		10min	3hr 45min	
dirt road (1680m)		55min	4hr 40min	
dirt road (1813m)		40min	5hr 20min	
Wolayerseehütte (1959m)	✓	40min	6hr	
Valentintörl (2138m)		45min	6hr 45min	
Gasthof Valentinalm (1220m)	✓	2hr 15min	9hr	
Stage 4A: Hochweißsteinhaus to Rifugio Marinelli			**8hr 50min**	**19.9**
Hochweißsteinhaus (1867m)	✓			

APPENDIX A – ROUTE BREAKDOWN

Key waypoints	Accommodation	Time (non-cumulative)	Time (cumulative)	Distance (km)
Öfner Joch (2011m)		20min	20min	
Casera Fleons di Sopra (1862m)		10min	30min	
Casera Fleons di Sotto (1576m)		50min	1hr 20min	
Casera Sissanis di Sotto (1684m)		40min	2hr	
Sella Sissanis (1987m)		1hr 15min	3hr 15min	
Passo di Niedergail (1994m)		20min	3hr 35min	
Giramondopass (2005m)		10min	3hr 45min	
dirt road (1680m)		55min	4hr 40min	
dirt road (1813m)		40min	5hr 20min	
Wolayerseehütte (1959m)	✓	40min	6hr	
Rifugio Lambertenghi Romanin (1955m)	✓	10min	6hr 10min	
grassy saddle (2230m)		1hr 40min	7hr 50min	
Rifugio Marinelli (2120m)	✓	1hr	8hr 50min	
Stage 5: Gasthof Valentinalm to Zollnerseehütte			**7hr 30min**	**19**
Gasthof Valentinalm (1220m)	✓			
Pöckenhaus (1215m)		45min	45min	
Untere Spielbodenalm (1453m)		1hr 5min	1hr 50min	
Obere Spielbodenalm (1835m)		40min	2hr 30min	

THE KARNISCHER HÖHENWEG

Key waypoints	Accommodation	Time (non-cumulative)	Time (cumulative)	Distance (km
Obere Tschintemuntalm (1812m)		45min	3hr 15min	
Ködertörl (2150m)		1hr 25min	4hr 40min	
Köder Alm (1831m)		30min	5hr 10min	
Obere Bischof Alm (1573m)		1hr 50min	7hr	
Zollnerseehütte (1738m)	✓	30min	7hr 30min	
Stage 5A: Rifugio Marinelli to Plöckenpass			**2hr 15min**	6.3
Rifugio Marinelli (2120m)	✓			
La Scaletta (1800m)		1hr	1hr	
Rio Collinetta (1690m)		15min	1hr 15min	
Plöckenpass (1360m)	✓	1hr	2hr 15min	
Stage 5B: Plöckenpass to Casera Pramosio			**7hr 15min**	11.2
Plöckenpass (1360m)	✓			
machine gun post (1480m)		20min	20min	
Kleiner Pal (1867m)		1hr 20min	1hr 40min	
Freikofelsattel (1617m)		1hr	2hr 40min	
Freikofel (1757m)		55min	3hr 35min	
Passo Cavallo (1581m)		40min	4hr 15min	
Casera di Palgrande di Sotto (1536m)		40min	4hr 55min	

Appendix A – Route breakdown

Key waypoints	Accommodation	Time (non-cumulative)	Time (cumulative)	Distance (km)
Casera di Palgrande di Sopra (1705m)		40min	5hr 35min	
Passo di Palgrande (1761m)		30min	6hr 5min	
Blausteinsattel (2101m)		50min	6hr 55min	
Casera Pramosio Alta (1940m)		20min	7hr 15min	
Casera Pramosio (1521m)	✓	20min	7hr 35min	
Stage 5C: Casera Pramosio to Zollnerseehütte			**3hr**	7
Casera Pramosio (1521m)	✓			
Passo Pramosio (1792m)		1hr	1hr	
Obere Bischof Alm (1573m)		1hr 30min	2hr 30min	
Zollnerseehütte (1738m)	✓	30min	3hr	
Stage 6: Zollnerseehütte to Alpenhof Plattner			**8hr 20min**	23.8
Zollnerseehütte (1738m)	✓			
Nölbling Pass (1817m)		20min	20min	
Waideggeralm-Sattel (1820m)		1hr	1hr 20min	
Straniger Alm (1479m)	✓	40min	2hr	
Sella di Cordin (1776m)		1hr	3hr	
Rattendorfer Sattel (1783m)		1hr	4hr	
Rudnigsattel (1940m)		2hr	6hr	

THE KARNISCHER HÖHENWEG

Key waypoints	Accommodation	Time (non-cumulative)	Time (cumulative)	Distance (km)
Tressdorfer Höhe (1869m)		1hr	7hr	
Nassfeldpass (1530m)	✓	1hr	8hr	
Alpenhof Plattner (1630m)	✓	20min	8hr 20min	26.6
Stage 7: Alpenhof Plattner to Gasthaus Starhand			**8hr 20min**	
Alpenhof Plattner (1630m)	✓			
Garnitzentörl (1873m)		50min	50min	
Garnitzenalm (1645m)		30min	1hr 20min	
Schultersattel (1432m)		40min	2hr	
Stallen Sattel (1496m)		15min	2hr 15min	
Kernitzenalm (1542m)		1hr 25min	3hr 40min	
Eggeralm (1422m)	✓	20min	4hr	
Dellacher Alm (1365m)		1hr	5hr	
Görtschacher Alm (1730m)		1hr 50min	6hr 50min	
Görtschacher Schneid (1885m)		30min	7hr 20min	
Gasthaus Starhand (1460m)	✓	1hr	8hr 20min	
Stage 8: Gasthaus Starhand to Arnoldstein			**8hr 30min**	28
Gasthaus Starhand (1460m)	✓			

Appendix A – Route breakdown

Key waypoints	Accommodation	Time (non-cumulative)	Time (cumulative)	Distance (km
Feistritzer Alm (1722m)	✓	1hr	1hr	
Achomitzer Alm (1715m)	✓	50min	1hr 50min	
Bartolo-Sattel (1175m)		1hr 30min	3hr 20min	
saddle (1685m)		1hr 30min	4hr 50min	
Göriacher Alm (1644m)		40min	5hr 30min	
birdwatching tower (1340m)		1hr	6hr 30min	
Thörl-Maglern (690m)		1hr	7hr 30min	
Arnoldstein (578m)	✓	1hr	8hr 30min	

APPENDIX B
Accommodation

Both Sillian and Sesto near the start of the walk have ATM machines and a full range of services. Arnoldstein, at the end of the walk, also has a full range of services.

Huts owned by the Austrian Alpine Club (Österreichischer Alpenverein, ÖAV) or the Italian Alpine Club (Club Alpino Italiano, CAI) are indicated below. Alpine Club members (including members of the British section of the Austrian Alpine Club) get a discount at these huts.

Stage 1
Alpenhotel Weitlanbrunn
tel +43 (0)4842 6655
www.weitlanbrunnosttirol.com

Hotel Schwarzer Adler
mob +43 (0)650 5307229
www.schwarzer-adler-sillian.com

Sillianer Hütte (ÖAV)
mob +43 (0)664 5323802
www.alpenverein.at/sillianerhuette

Obstanserseehütte (ÖAV)
tel +43 (0)4848 5422
www.alpenverein.at/obstanserseehuette

Stage 2
Standschützenhütte (ÖAV)
mob +43 (0)664 1127153
(contact only by SMS)
www.alpenverein.at/filmoorstandschuetzenhuette

Porzehütte (ÖAV)
mob +43 (0)664 3256452
www.alpenverein.at/porzehuette

Stage 3
Hochweißsteinhaus (ÖAV)
mob +43 (0)676 7462886
www.alpenverein.at/hochweisssteinhaus

Stage 4
Wolayerseehütte (ÖAV)
tel +43 (0)720 346141
www.wolayerseehuette-lesachtal.at

Rifugio Lambertenghi Romanin (CAI)
tel +39 0433 786074
www.rifugiolambertenghi.it

Gasthof Valentinalm
tel +43 (0)4715 92215
www.valentinalm.at

Stage 4A
Rifugio Marinelli (CAI)
tel +39 0433 779177
www.rifugiomarinelli.com

Stage 5
Zollnerseehütte (ÖAV)
mob +43 (0)676 9602209
www.alpenverein.at/zollnerseehuette

Stage 5A
Albergo Al Valico
tel +39 0433 779326

Gasthof Valentinalm
see Stage 4

Appendix C – Useful contacts

Stage 5B
Casera Pramosio
tel +39 0433 775757

Stage 5C
Zollnerseehütte (ÖAV)
see Stage 5

Stage 6
Straniger Alm
mob +43 (0)680 2220262
www.straniger-alm.at

Berghof Nassfeld
tel +43 (0)4285 8271
www.berghof.or.at

Alpenhof Plattner
tel +43 (0)4285 8285
www.plattner.at

Stage 7
Gasthaus zum Rudi
mob +43 (0)676 9343605
www.zumrudi.at

Gasthaus Starhand
tel +43 (0)4283 2004
mob (0)664 9470231

Stage 8
Gasthaus Oisternig
mob +43 (0)699 17242520

Schönwipfel-Schutzhaus
mob +43 (0)664 11410579

Hotel und Genusswirt Wallner
tel +43 (0)4255 2356

APPENDIX C
Useful contacts

Walking information

The Austrian Alpine Club website (see below) is an excellent source of information and includes all you need to know about finding and staying in a hut. It is worth checking the site as you plan your trip, since the approach to booking is developing all the time. The individual hut websites typically include information on the local network of routes and how long it takes to get from one hut to another.

Alpine Club membership
Austrian Alpine Club (British Section – but all 'overseas members' can apply)
www.aacuk.org.uk

Navigation
The Viewranger GPS app runs on Apple and Android smartphones and maps can be purchased at their online store: www.viewranger.com.

Paper maps
The Map Shop
15 High Street
Upton-upon-Severn
Worcs
WR8 0HJ
www.themapshop.co.uk

THE KARNISCHER HÖHENWEG

Stanfords
12–14 Long Acre
London
WC2E 9LP
www.stanfords.co.uk

Transport

Most people will combine flights with either trains or buses to get to and from the walk. With a wide range of destinations to choose from (Innsbruck, Salzburg, Munich, Vienna, Venice and Ljubljana), the airport of departure is likely to be an important consideration.

For multi-mode transport planning from anywhere to anywhere, try www.rome2rio.com. Although the information provided is not completely reliable, it is a good starting point.

Air

Easyjet
www.easyjet.com

Ryanair
www.ryanair.com

Rail

For advice on rail travel, go to:
www.seat61.com.

Österreichische Bundesbahnen (Austria)
www.oebb.at

Trenitalia (Italy)
www.trenitalia.com

Bus

In Italy and the Dolomites, bus/coach travel is particularly relevant – the most important operator is Dolomiti Bus:
www.dolomitibus.it.

Emergency and health

In the mountains, mobile phone coverage is patchy. If you can get a connection, help should be available in English on the European emergency number 112.

DOWNLOAD THE ROUTE IN GPX FORMAT

All the stages in this guide are available for download as GPX files from:

www.cicerone.co.uk/942/GPX

You should be able to load them into most formats
of mobile device, whether GPS or smartphone.
When you go to this link, you will be asked for your email address and where you purchased the guide, and have the option to subscribe to the Cicerone e-newsletter.

CICERONE
www.cicerone.co.uk

LISTING OF CICERONE GUIDES

SCOTLAND

Backpacker's Britain: Northern Scotland
Ben Nevis and Glen Coe
Cycling in the Hebrides
Great Mountain Days in Scotland
Mountain Biking in Southern and Central Scotland
Mountain Biking in West and North West Scotland
Not the West Highland Way Scotland
Scotland's Best Small Mountains
Scotland's Far West
Scotland's Mountain Ridges
Scrambles in Lochaber
The Ayrshire and Arran Coastal Paths
The Border Country
The Cape Wrath Trail
The Great Glen Way
The Great Glen Way Map Booklet
The Hebridean Way
The Hebrides
The Isle of Mull
The Isle of Skye
The Skye Trail
The Southern Upland Way
The Speyside Way
The Speyside Way Map Booklet
The West Highland Way
Walking Highland Perthshire
Walking in Scotland's Far North
Walking in the Angus Glens
Walking in the Cairngorms
Walking in the Ochils, Campsie Fells and Lomond Hills
Walking in the Pentland Hills
Walking in the Southern Uplands
Walking in Torridon
Walking Loch Lomond and the Trossachs
Walking on Arran
Walking on Harris and Lewis
Walking on Jura, Islay and Colonsay
Walking on Rum and the Small Isles
Walking on the Orkney and Shetland Isles
Walking on Uist and Barra
Walking the Corbetts Vol 1 South of the Great Glen
Walking the Corbetts Vol 2 North of the Great Glen
Walking the Galloway Hills
Walking the Munros Vol 1 – Southern, Central and Western Highlands
Walking the Munros Vol 2 – Northern Highlands and the Cairngorms
West Highland Way Map Booklet
Winter Climbs Ben Nevis and Glen Coe
Winter Climbs in the Cairngorms

NORTHERN ENGLAND TRAILS

Hadrian's Wall Path
Hadrian's Wall Path Map Booklet
Pennine Way Map Booklet
The Coast to Coast Map Booklet
The Coast to Coast Walk
The Dales Way
The Dales Way Map Booklet
The Pennine Way

LAKE DISTRICT

Cycling in the Lake District
Great Mountain Days in the Lake District
Lake District Winter Climbs
Lake District: High Level and Fell Walks
Lake District: Low Level and Lake Walks
Lakeland Fellranger
Mountain Biking in the Lake District
Scrambles in the Lake District – North and South
Short Walks in Lakeland Book 1: South Lakeland
Short Walks in Lakeland Book 2: North Lakeland
Short Walks in Lakeland Book 3: West Lakeland
Tour of the Lake District
Trail and Fell Running in the Lake District

NORTH WEST ENGLAND AND THE ISLE OF MAN

Cycling the Pennine Bridleway
Cycling the Way of the Roses
Isle of Man Coastal Path
The Lancashire Cycleway
The Lune Valley and Howgills
The Ribble Way
Walking in Cumbria's Eden Valley
Walking in Lancashire
Walking in the Forest of Bowland and Pendle
Walking on the Isle of Man
Walking on the West Pennine Moors
Walks in Lancashire Witch Country
Walks in Ribble Country
Walks in Silverdale and Arnside

NORTH EAST ENGLAND, YORKSHIRE DALES AND PENNINES

Cycling in the Yorkshire Dales
Great Mountain Days in the Pennines
Mountain Biking in the Yorkshire Dales
South Pennine Walks
St Oswald's Way and St Cuthbert's Way
The Cleveland Way and the Yorkshire Wolds Way
The Cleveland Way Map Booklet
The North York Moors
The Reivers Way
The Teesdale Way
Walking in County Durham
Walking in Northumberland
Walking in the North Pennines
Walking in the Yorkshire Dales: North and East
Walking in the Yorkshire Dales: South and West
Walks in Dales Country
Walks in the Yorkshire Dales

WALES AND WELSH BORDERS

Glyndwr's Way
Great Mountain Days in Snowdonia
Hillwalking in Shropshire
Hillwalking in Wales – Vol 1
Hillwalking in Wales – Vol 2
Mountain Walking in Snowdonia
Offa's Dyke Path
Offa's Dyke Map Booklet
Pembrokeshire Coast Path Map Booklet
Ridges of Snowdonia
Scrambles in Snowdonia
The Ascent of Snowdon
The Ceredigion and Snowdonia Coast Paths
The Pembrokeshire Coast Path
The Severn Way
The Snowdonia Way
The Wales Coast Path
The Wye Valley Walk
Walking in Carmarthenshire
Walking in Pembrokeshire
Walking in the Forest of Dean
Walking in the South Wales Valleys
Walking in the Wye Valley
Walking on the Brecon Beacons
Walking on the Gower
Welsh Winter Climbs

DERBYSHIRE, PEAK DISTRICT AND MIDLANDS

Cycling in the Peak District
Dark Peak Walks
Scrambles in the Dark Peak
Walking in Derbyshire
White Peak Walks: The Northern Dales
White Peak Walks: The Southern Dales

SOUTHERN ENGLAND

20 Classic Sportive Rides in South East England
20 Classic Sportive Rides in South West England
Cycling in the Cotswolds
Mountain Biking on the North Downs
Mountain Biking on the South Downs
North Downs Way Map Booklet
South West Coast Path Map Booklet – Minehead to St Ives
South West Coast Path Map Booklet – Plymouth to Poole
South West Coast Path Map Booklet – St Ives to Plymouth
Suffolk Coast and Heath Walks
The Cotswold Way
The Cotswold Way Map Booklet
The Great Stones Way
The Kennet and Avon Canal
The Lea Valley Walk
The North Downs Way
The Peddars Way and Norfolk Coast Path
The Pilgrims' Way
The Ridgeway Map Booklet
The Ridgeway National Trail
The South Downs Way
The South Downs Way Map Booklet
The South West Coast Path
The Thames Path
The Thames Path Map Booklet
The Two Moors Way
Walking Hampshire's Test Way
Walking in Cornwall
Walking in Essex
Walking in Kent
Walking in London
Walking in Norfolk
Walking in Sussex
Walking in the Chilterns
Walking in the Cotswolds
Walking in the Isles of Scilly
Walking in the New Forest
Walking in the North Wessex Downs
Walking in the Thames Valley
Walking on Dartmoor
Walking on Guernsey
Walking on Jersey
Walking on the Isle of Wight
Walking on the Jurassic Coast
Walks in the South Downs National Park

BRITISH ISLES CHALLENGES, COLLECTIONS AND ACTIVITIES

The Book of the Bivvy
The Book of the Bothy
The C2C Cycle Route
The End to End Cycle Route
The Mountains of England and Wales: Vol 1 Wales
The Mountains of England and Wales: Vol 2 England
The National Trails
The UK's County Tops
Three Peaks, Ten Tors

ALPS CROSS-BORDER ROUTES

100 Hut Walks in the Alps
Across the Eastern Alps: E5
Alpine Ski Mountaineering Vol 1 – Western Alps
Alpine Ski Mountaineering Vol 2 – Central and Eastern Alps
Chamonix to Zermatt
The Karnischer Höhenweg
The Tour of the Bernina
Tour of Mont Blanc
Tour of Monte Rosa
Tour of the Matterhorn
Trail Running – Chamonix and the Mont Blanc region
Trekking in the Alps
Trekking in the Silvretta and Rätikon Alps
Trekking Munich to Venice
Walking in the Alps

PYRENEES AND FRANCE/SPAIN CROSS-BORDER ROUTES

The GR10 Trail
The GR11 Trail
The Pyrenean Haute Route
The Pyrenees
The Way of St James – Spain
Walks and Climbs in the Pyrenees

AUSTRIA

The Adlerweg
Trekking in Austria's Hohe Tauern
Trekking in the Stubai Alps
Trekking in the Zillertal Alps
Walking in Austria

SWITZERLAND

Cycle Touring in Switzerland
The Swiss Alpine Pass Route – Via Alpina Route 1
The Swiss Alps
Tour of the Jungfrau Region
Walking in the Bernese Oberland
Walking in the Valais
Walks in the Engadine – Switzerland

FRANCE AND BELGIUM

Chamonix Mountain Adventures
Cycle Touring in France
Cycling London to Paris
Cycling the Canal du Midi
Écrins National Park
Mont Blanc Walks
Mountain Adventures in the Maurienne
The GR20 Corsica
The GR5 Trail
The GR5 Trail – Vosges and Jura
The Grand Traverse of the Massif Central
The Loire Cycle Route
The Moselle Cycle Route
The River Rhone Cycle Route
The Robert Louis Stevenson Trail
The Way of St James
Tour of the Oisans: The GR54
Tour of the Queyras
Tour of the Vanoise
Vanoise Ski Touring
Via Ferratas of the French Alps
Walking in Corsica
Walking in Provence – East
Walking in Provence – West
Walking in the Auvergne
Walking in the Briançonnais
Walking in the Cevennes
Walking in the Dordogne
Walking in the Haute Savoie: North
Walking in the Haute Savoie: South
Walks in the Cathar Region
Walking in the Ardennes

GERMANY

Hiking and Biking in the Black Forest
The Danube Cycleway Volume 1
The Rhine Cycle Route
The Westweg
Walking in the Bavarian Alps

ICELAND AND GREENLAND

Trekking in Greenland
Walking and Trekking in Iceland

IRELAND
The Irish Coast to Coast Walk
The Mountains of Ireland
The Wild Atlantic Way and Western Ireland

ITALY
Italy's Sibillini National Park
Shorter Walks in the Dolomites
Ski Touring and Snowshoeing in the Dolomites
The Way of St Francis
Through the Italian Alps
Trekking in the Apennines
Trekking in the Dolomites
Via Ferratas of the Italian Dolomites Vol 1
Via Ferratas of the Italian Dolomites: Vol 2
Walking and Trekking in the Gran Paradiso
Walking in Abruzzo
Walking in Italy's Stelvio National Park
Walking in Sardinia
Walking in Sicily
Walking in the Dolomites
Walking in Tuscany
Walking in Umbria
Walking on the Amalfi Coast
Walking the Italian Lakes
Walks and Treks in the Maritime Alps

SCANDINAVIA: NORWAY, SWEDEN, FINLAND
Walking in Norway

EASTERN EUROPE AND THE BALKANS
The Danube Cycleway Volume 2
The High Tatras
The Mountains of Romania
Walking in Bulgaria's National Parks
Walking in Hungary
Mountain Biking in Slovenia
The Islands of Croatia
The Julian Alps of Slovenia
The Mountains of Montenegro
The Peaks of the Balkans Trail
Trekking in Slovenia
Walking in Croatia
Walking in Slovenia: The Karavanke

SPAIN
Coastal Walks in Andalucia
Cycle Touring in Spain
Mountain Walking in Mallorca
Mountain Walking in Southern Catalunya
Spain's Sendero Histórico: The GR1
The Andalucian Coast to Coast Walk
The Mountains of Nerja
The Mountains of Ronda and Grazalema
The Northern Caminos
The Sierras of Extremadura
The Way of St James Cyclist Guide
Trekking in Mallorca
Walking and Trekking in the Sierra Nevada
Walking in Andalucia
Walking in Menorca
Walking in the Cordillera Cantabrica
Walking on Gran Canaria
Walking on La Gomera and El Hierro
Walking on La Palma
Walking on Lanzarote and Fuerteventura
Walking on Tenerife
Walking on the Costa Blanca

PORTUGAL
The Camino Portugués
Walking in Portugal
Walking in the Algarve

GREECE, CYPRUS AND MALTA
The High Mountains of Crete
Trekking in Greece
Walking and Trekking on Corfu
Walking in Cyprus
Walking on Malta

INTERNATIONAL CHALLENGES, COLLECTIONS AND ACTIVITIES
Canyoning in the Alps
The Via Francigena Canterbury to Rome – Parts 1 and 2

AFRICA
Climbing in the Moroccan Anti-Atlas
Mountaineering in the Moroccan High Atlas
The High Atlas
Trekking in the Atlas Mountains
Kilimanjaro
Walking in the Drakensberg

JORDAN
Jordan – Walks, Treks, Caves, Climbs and Canyons
Treks and Climbs in Wadi Rum, Jordan

ASIA
Annapurna
Everest: A Trekker's Guide
Trekking in the Himalaya
Trekking in Bhutan
Trekking in Ladakh
The Mount Kailash Trek

USA AND CANADA
British Columbia
The John Muir Trail
The Pacific Crest Trail

ARGENTINA, CHILE AND PERU
Aconcagua and the Southern Andes
Hiking and Biking Peru's Inca Trails
Torres del Paine

TECHNIQUES
Geocaching in the UK
Indoor Climbing
Lightweight Camping
Map and Compass
Outdoor Photography
Polar Exploration
Rock Climbing
Sport Climbing
The Mountain Hut Book

MINI GUIDES
Alpine Flowers
Avalanche!
Navigation
Pocket First Aid and Wilderness Medicine
Snow

MOUNTAIN LITERATURE
8000 metres
A Walk in the Clouds
Abode of the Gods
The Pennine Way – the Path, the People, the Journey
Unjustifiable Risk?

For full information on all our guides, books and eBooks, visit our website:
www.cicerone.co.uk

Walking – Trekking – Mountaineering – Climbing – Cycling

Over 40 years, Cicerone have built up an outstanding collection of over 300 guides, inspiring all sorts of amazing adventures.

Every guide comes from extensive exploration and research by our expert authors, all with a passion for their subjects. They are frequently praised, endorsed and used by clubs, instructors and outdoor organisations.

All our titles can now be bought as **e-books**, **ePubs** and **Kindle** files and we also have an online magazine – **Cicerone Extra** – with features to help cyclists, climbers, walkers and trekkers choose their next adventure, at home or abroad.

Our website shows any **new information** we've had in since a book was published. Please do let us know if you find anything has changed, so that we can publish the latest details. On our **website** you'll also find great ideas and lots of detailed information about what's inside every guide and you can buy **individual routes** from many of them online.

It's easy to keep in touch with what's going on at Cicerone by getting our monthly **free e-newsletter**, which is full of offers, competitions, up-to-date information and topical articles. You can subscribe on our home page and also follow us on **Facebook** and **Twitter** or dip into our **blog**.

Cicerone – the very best guides for exploring the world.

CICERONE

Juniper House, Murley Moss, Oxenholme Road, Kendal, Cumbria LA9 7RL
Tel: 015395 62069 info@cicerone.co.uk
www.cicerone.co.uk